MATH SENSE

The Look, Sound, and Feel of Effective Instruction

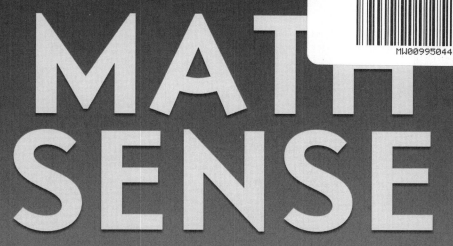

Stenhouse Publishers • Portland, Maine

Christine Moynihan

Stenhouse Publishers
www.stenhouse.com

Library of Congress Cataloging-in-Publication Data
Moynihan, Christine, 1951–
    Math sense : the look, sound, and feel of effective instruction /
Christine Moynihan.
        page cm
        Includes bibliographical references.
        ISBN 978-1-57110-942-2 (pbk. : alk. paper)—ISBN (invalid) 978-1-57110-979-8 (ebook) 1. Mathematics—Study and teaching—Standards.
2. Effective teaching. I. Title.
        QA11.2.M69 2012
        510.71--dc23
                                                            2012029983

Cover design, interior design, and typesetting by Martha Drury

Manufactured in the United States of America

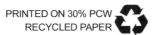
PRINTED ON 30% PCW
RECYCLED PAPER

18 17 16 15 14 13   9 8 7 6 5 4 3 2

*To all who strive to bring the wonder, beauty,
and joy of math to children!*

CONTENTS

ACKNOWLEDGMENTS

It may not take a village, but it does take a number of people to write a book. As a result of my thirty-plus years in education, I have been fortunate enough to be touched by many who have affected my thinking and made me wonder and question and reflect. These include incredibly generous teachers, amazingly supportive administrators, and, most important, scores of the very best "teachers" of all—the extraordinary children who have come in and out of my life. I would have nothing to write about if not for all of them.

Specific thanks go to the students and teachers of the Foster, Plymouth River, and South elementary schools in Hingham, Massachusetts. They allowed me to be present in their rooms to observe and capture images of deep and meaningful mathematics teaching and learning. The same holds true for the students and teachers at Jaworek Elementary School in Marlborough, Massachusetts—their excitement about learning is palpable and gives me great hope for the future!

I am also fortunate to have been surrounded by a group of women who have been mentors, sounding boards, and, most of all, friends. Mimi, my first cooperating teacher and dear friend these many years later—you taught me so much about the art of teaching and always made me want to do my best. I tried to emulate both you and Elaine, another master cooperating teacher, and absorb and incorporate as much as I could. You started me on the right path and have been there ever since to share the journey. Blake, when I first met you, you were a classroom teacher and I was the district math specialist, and I knew right away that we would be forever linked. I saw in you this insatiable love of math, and I took advantage of that by pulling you into the vortex! Your sphere of influence has grown since then, as you are now a phenomenal math specialist, and I still take advantage of you and your expertise every chance I get (I could not have done this book without you!). To another dear friend (and math specialist), known as L-Squared (due to her alliterative name)—you are as crazy as the rest of us and a cheerleader all the way. And Debbie—your unfailing, unwavering, unrelenting belief in me, as well as your countless hours of talking me through this process, allowed me to complete this task. You kept telling me I was almost there—almost at Heartbreak Hill—and that I could do the rest, that I could make it even when I wanted to give up. (For those of you familiar with the Boston Marathon, you know that Heartbreak Hill is between miles 20 and 21 on the 26.2-mile route, and it is the point where energy is flagging and muscles are screaming—this is where you need the supportive voices pushing and pulling you to the finish line.) Thank you, one and all!

To my editor, Toby Gordon—you introduced me to the Stenhouse family, and I am forever a fan. Your quiet guidance and consistent support helped me in all of the rough spots—you have my deep appreciation.

As the oldest of nine children, I grew up in a loud, boisterous, and extraordinary family. Our parents gave us unconditional love and embedded within us the belief that we were each blessed—and we were. We still are, in fact, because not only do we love each other, we also like each other—always have and always will. I have been further blessed with my own husband and children who have accepted, understood, and supported my passion in every way. How lucky can a person be? My love forever to Brian, Caitlin, and Kevin—you are my rocks, my anchors, my loves!

CHAPTER 1

WHAT IS MATHEMATICS?

I f you are reading this book, you are likely among the growing number of teachers who believe that mathematics is much more than memorizing and spilling out "learned" definitions and procedures—that it can, should, and must be accessible to all students. You likely see mathematics as a way of processing information—analyzing, organizing, hypothesizing, representing, modeling, justifying—all in the pursuit of solving problems. You likely know that computational speed is not *the* defining mark of a good mathematical thinker. Further, you likely believe that teaching mathematics makes a difference in how your students view mathematics and how they view themselves as mathematical learners. This is an awesome responsibility and a never-ending journey. We continuously work to improve our teaching so that our students' learning improves.

Principles and Standards for School Mathematics (National Council of Teachers of Mathematics 2000) and *Curriculum Focal Points for Prekindergarten Through Grade 8 Mathematics* (National Council of Teachers of Mathematics 2006) help answer the question, "What is mathematics?" These documents provide a framework for looking at mathematics as the integration of content and processes and outline a path for getting there. *Principles and Standards for School Mathematics* sets forth a rigorous and comprehensive set of goals for attaining meaningful and high-quality curriculum for all students; *Curriculum Focal Points for Prekindergarten Through Grade 8 Mathematics* specifies the instructional progression within and across grade-level bands of concepts and how to teach them so that greater understanding results.

The Common Core State Standards Initiative, a state-led effort coordinated by the National Governors Association for Best Practices and the Council of Chief State School Officers, released a set of standards (CCSSI 2010) that serves as another signpost for a richer vision of math. The major goal of this effort is to articulate both the knowledge and the skills in English language arts and in mathematics that all students should master during their K–12 schooling. The Common Core's subtitle captures the mission succinctly: "Preparing America's Students for College and Career." After thirteen years in our schools, students should be ready to enter either college or the workforce equipped with all that they need to be successful.

All of us in education are on a journey, and every step makes us better at our jobs. This book is focused on mathematics teaching and learning and is meant to help you do that job by heightening your math sense and by providing an overview of some of the elements—the seeds—that should be seen, heard, and felt in elementary mathematics instruction in twenty-first-century classrooms. This book is not meant as the be-all and end-all reference; it is meant as a resource for new and veteran teachers as well as administrators to help you look at, listen to, and feel what is happening in your mathematics instruction, identify what you are already doing well, and select a few elements for deeper focus. It is a compilation of some of what I have learned from administrators, teachers, and students. Even though I continue to learn every time I am in a classroom, I hope you will benefit from my sharing and that you will find yourself nodding your head in agreement at various points as well as having an occasional "Hmm . . . interesting" moment.

Although good mathematics teaching cannot be reduced to identifying key elements and checking them off a list, there are essential elements of mathematics teaching that can and should be seen, heard, and felt. I explain some of these elements while magnifying what mathematics should look like, amplifying what it should sound like, and intensifying what it should feel like so that you can use this information to assess, inform, and refine your practice.

Chapter 2, "The Look of the Landscape," explores the physical space, or landscape, of the classroom and identifies some of the "things" that can make teaching mathematics richer. The presence of these elements doesn't automatically improve teaching and learning, but, if they are used properly, consistently, and meaningfully, students will benefit. Therefore, I discuss aspects of the physical classroom landscape in terms of what they are, why they are useful, and where we use them.

Chapter 3, "The Look of the Lesson: Teachers," focuses on elements teachers use during a mathematics lesson. Chapter 4, "The Look of the Lesson: Students," illustrates how students engage in and work on mathematics. As with Chapter 3, each element is examined for what it is, why it is useful, and when or where we use it.

Chapter 5, "The Sound of the Lesson," highlights some of the elements that should be heard during math instructional time. Whether you have been teaching for one year or twenty years, you recognize that math instruction involves teachers who support discourse and engage students as well as students who analyze and clarify their thinking. This chapter brings these elements into sharper focus.

Chapter 6, "The Feel of It All," explores elements that are difficult to identify, challenging to detect, and tough to teach. They are intangible yet palpable. These are the things that you just *feel* and that add to the overall spirit of the classroom. These affective pieces are powerful motivators and add an important dimension to mathematics teaching and learning.

Chapter 7, "Putting It Together," suggests how to use what you've discovered in this book. Change is a continuous process, and it is not always easy. My basic advice to you is to start small with some manageable yet significant changes and build from there. I provide here an overview of some steps that can be useful as you move forward to improve your teaching.

Father Stanley Bezuszka of Boston College, a wonderful mentor, inspired many budding teachers by sharing the joy involved in teaching mathematics to children. One of his many quotes still resonates:

Mathematics is like a pomegranate—there are delightful tidbits every-where. You break it and at first nothing is visible and then you remove a thin layer of skin and there are the seeds—a delightful surprise and a pleasure. (Bezuszka 1993, 15)

Let's start on this journey and unwrap that pomegranate together as we explore opportunities, challenges, and excitement—finding the "delightful tidbits"—we experience along the way.

CHAPTER 2

THE LOOK OF
THE LANDSCAPE

*Few enterprises of great labor or hazard would be undertaken if we had
not the power of magnifying the advantages we expect from them.*

—Samuel Johnson

Picture this: you are entering a second-grade classroom—not your own—for the very first time. It is October, and, as you take your first step inside, you stop for a moment and look. You see four students on the floor near the door playing a math card game. Five students are on the rug in the corner with Judy clocks, focusing on time (this exploration works well with a parent volunteer if you have one but also works with students directing themselves). Six students are in the area labeled "Math Center" talking and working in pairs on a journal or workbook. The teacher is at the back of the room at a kidney-shaped table with a small group of students, leading a discussion about problem-solving strategies displaying several sets of problems at varying levels of difficulty. Four students wearing headsets are working independently on a computer program that supports number facts fluency. Four other students are on the rug at the front of the room where there is a whiteboard, a chart stand, and an interactive whiteboard: two are using virtual base ten blocks and the other two are using actual base ten blocks to complete a recording sheet. Purposeful activity is visible in every nook and cranny. You notice in various areas of the room a daily agenda with starting and ending times, a list of mathematical goals for the day, a number line around the perimeter of the room, a math word wall, a math games station, various manipulatives in labeled clear containers, and a student-created bulletin board with favorite numbers named multiple ways. So much to look at; so much to see.

While looks are not everything, they can certainly help give an important first impression. When you walk into a store for the first time, you can sense in the first minute or so, by looking at the displays, the merchandise, the salespeople, or the fixtures, whether it will become a favorite shopping destination. When you visit a friend's new home for the first time, you gain immediate information about her tastes from the colors of the walls, the artwork, the furniture arrangement, and the treasures displayed on the tables. Similarly, when you enter a classroom for the first time, you gain an enormous amount of information. You learn what is valued. You discern what happens within its walls by taking in the "look" of the classroom.

Whether you are an administrator, a new classroom teacher, or an experienced teacher assigned to a new grade level or returning to the same grade level, you know by way of instinct and/or experience the value of setting up a classroom so that it "speaks" with purpose. With an eye toward things mathematical, let's unpack and magnify some of the components that compose the physical landscape of a classroom. Each component will be magnified to highlight the *what, why,* and *where* and to set in context the important elements of mathematics instruction. Of course, these are not the only significant components. You most likely can add many others, which is what makes teaching interesting and dynamic. I am only discussing elements that convey the high regard mathematics occupies and its meaningful role in your classroom. They include the following:

1. Number line
2. One hundred chart/number grid
3. Manipulatives collection
4. Student work samples
5. Daily schedule

6. Designated mathematics center/area
7. Mathematics word wall
8. Mathematics literature collection
9. Technology
10. Multiple instructional settings

1. NUMBER LINE

▶ *What*

A number line is a representation of numbers as points on a line. Two types of number lines are useful in the classroom—while the horizontal one (Figure 2.1) is most often seen, consider displaying a vertical one (Figure 2.2) as well. Both should contain negative numbers, and the horizontal one should extend at least to numeral 180 for all K–5 classrooms. Student-sized number lines can be used on desks and worktables.

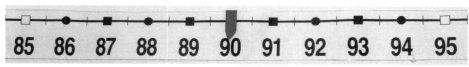

Figure 2.1: A horizontal number line that starts with negative numbers and extends to 180 is an important classroom resource.

▶ *Why*

The purposes of a number line are

- to provide a linear representation of numbers;
- to serve as a manipulative for computation, ordering of numbers, and visualization of common ("friendly") fractions; and
- to furnish both a concrete and a pictorial representation of the number system that evolves into a mental model.

▶ *Where*

Having a horizontal number line along the perimeter of the classroom is a powerful teaching and learning tool. It can be placed above whiteboards or chalkboards, but it is especially helpful if students can reach it. Place a vertical number line where students typically gather for whole-class instruction, such as on the rug or other meeting area.

Figure 2.2: Vertical number lines offer another view of positive and negative numbers.

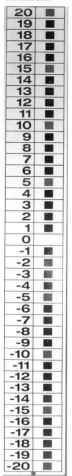

▶ *Magnification*

Elementary teachers, particularly teachers of kindergarten through grade two—and maybe even into grade three—know the importance of a number line. It presents obvious counting opportunities for younger grades—counting (while pointing) in unison by ones, twos, etc., both forward and backward. The number line illustrates connections to friendly fractions. ("Today is Day 88 in the school year—about _____ or $\frac{1}{2}$ of the way through the year.") The number line provides a way to model mental addition and subtraction. ("If we start at 22 and add 3, where are we?") In addition, you can play such number games as "number squeeze," as in this kindergarten classroom.

Ms. Melendez: I am thinking of a number.
Melinda: Is it 30?
Ms. Melendez: It is less than 30. (She places a transparent overlay on 30 on the number line under the marker tray.)
Anthony: Is it 15?
Ms. Melendez: It is greater than 15. (She places an overlay on 15.)

Play continues until the students have "squeezed" enough to identify the number. The number line is a problem-solving tool, helping students see the results of their guesses, the effect of their reasoning, and the relationship of numbers. Figure 2.3 shows a group of kindergartners playing the number squeeze game on their own.

Number lines are important for *every* elementary classroom, even upper grades. The same types of activities that play well in lower elementary grades also play well in the upper grades, with, of course, more complex number situations. Let's take a look at how a fourth-grade class uses number lines.

Mr. Butler: Harry earned $10 for raking leaves for a neighbor. He owed his mother $15, so he gave her his earnings. What's his status now and how do you know?
Elias: He's $5 in the hole or really at −5. Look. (He moves to the vertical number line at the front of the class.) He started here (pointing to −15), and he made $10, so now he's here (pointing to −5).
Mr. Butler: Who is following Elias's thinking? (Mr. Butler waits until several hands are raised.) Who can elaborate?
Jemini: Elias said that Harry started at −15 (pointing to the number line) because that's what he owed his mother and he has to pay it back. So when he earned the ten dollars, he moved up ten places closer to the

Figure 2.3: These four kindergartners are enjoying a student-led number-squeeze activity, refining their skills at identifying an unknown number.

good side—the positive side. He doesn't get there all the way because when you're at −15 and you add 10, you only get to −5.

Mr. Butler: I see what you're saying, Jemini. Elias, does Jemini's explanation match what you are thinking?

Elias: Yeah. If you're in debt, it's negative and you move to the left on a number line, so Harry was at −15. If you earn money, it's positive and you move to the right. He got closer to paying off his mother. (He moves up ten spaces on the number line and stops at −5.) He didn't make it all the way, but now he only owes her $5.

Mr. Butler: Great explanation! Can anyone give the number sentence that matches this?

Here again the number line provides both a teaching and a learning tool for problem solving and allows students to use a visual representation to compute with positive and negative integers in an accessible and contextualized setting. So, upper elementary teachers, grab those number lines from the supply shelves and get them up on the walls. Yes, I know it's often quite a challenge positioning them around doors, windows, bulletin boards and then making them stick! The benefits are well worth the effort, so keep taping, gluing, and pasting—whatever it takes.

2. ONE HUNDRED CHART/NUMBER GRID

◗ *What*

A 100 chart is often called a number grid. It's really a number line that stops at 100 (usually), is shaped into a 10-by-10 square (see Figure 2.4), and is most often posted on a wall. The most common number line starts at 1 and ends at 100; however, it can start at 0 and stop at either 99 or 100 (see Figure 2.5). Both forms are useful and serve similar purposes. Another type of number grid continues to 200 or beyond (see Figure 2.6). In addition, a 100-pocket chart is helpful in K–2 classrooms (see Figure 2.7).

◗ *Why*

The purposes of a 100 chart are

- to provide a visual model of oral and choral counting (by 1s, 2s, 3s, etc.),
- to present a visual representation of patterns in our number system,
- to serve as a manipulative for computation (student-sized), and
- to highlight the iterative nature of our number system (how elements repeat and can be used to see patterns and relationships).

◗ *Where*

While 100 charts can be placed throughout the classroom, it makes sense to put at least one where students gather away from their desks for whole-class instruction purposes. It also makes sense to have a basket of student-sized number grids available for quick access.

◗ *Magnification*

Hundred charts and pocket charts, useful at all levels, are especially valuable at K–2 as students begin to explore the number system and notice patterns.

1	2	3	4	5	6	7	8	9	10
11	12	13	14	15	16	17	18	19	20
21	22	23	24	25	26	27	28	29	30
31	32	33	34	35	36	37	38	39	40
41	42	43	44	45	46	47	48	49	50
51	52	53	54	55	56	57	58	59	60
61	62	63	64	65	66	67	68	69	70
71	72	73	74	75	76	77	78	79	80
81	82	83	84	85	86	87	88	89	90
91	92	93	94	95	96	97	98	99	100

Figure 2.4: This number grid offers one way to arrange the numbers from 1 to 100.

0–99 Chart

0	1	2	3	4	5	6	7	8	9
10	11	12	13	14	15	16	17	18	19
20	21	22	23	24	25	26	27	28	29
30	31	32	33	34	35	36	37	38	39
40	41	42	43	44	45	46	47	48	49
50	51	52	53	54	55	56	57	58	59
60	61	62	63	64	65	66	67	68	69
70	71	72	73	74	75	76	77	78	79
80	81	82	83	84	85	86	87	88	89
90	91	92	93	94	95	96	97	98	99

Figure 2.5: The 0–99 number grid provides a chance to look for different patterns.

Numbers from 1 to 200

1	2	3	4	5	6	7	8	9	10
11	12	13	14	15	16	17	18	19	20
21	22	23	24	25	26	27	28	29	30
31	32	33	34	35	36	37	38	39	40
41	42	43	44	45	46	47	48	49	50
51	52	53	54	55	56	57	58	59	60
61	62	63	64	65	66	67	68	69	70
71	72	73	74	75	76	77	78	79	80
81	82	83	84	85	86	87	88	89	90
91	92	93	94	95	96	97	98	99	100
101	102	103	104	105	106	107	108	109	110
111	112	113	114	115	116	117	118	119	120
121	122	123	124	125	126	127	128	129	130
131	132	133	134	135	136	137	138	139	140
141	142	143	144	145	146	147	148	149	150
151	152	153	154	155	156	157	158	159	160
161	162	163	164	165	166	167	168	169	170
171	172	173	174	175	176	177	178	179	180
181	182	183	184	185	186	187	188	189	190
191	192	193	194	195	196	197	198	199	200

Figure 2.6: A 200-number grid allows students to see how number patterns continue past 100.

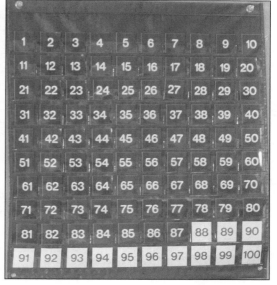

Figure 2.7: A 100-pocket chart on the 87th day of school

Some pocket charts come with two-sided numbered cards of different colors or transparent squares that fit over the numbers. These can be helpful in group oral counting to highlight counting patterns (even and odd numbers, 2s, 5s, 10s). Transparent squares also fit into the number slots to reinforce counting, sequencing, and recognizing patterns. The laminated 100 charts are also good to have. When they are accessible on a classroom wall and in a smaller size on student desks or tables, they can serve both as a reference and a problem-solving tool.

A number grid in K–2 classrooms should continue beyond 100. Too often, young children think our number system stops at 100. Those of you who have listened to a child count to 100 and then stop, as if he has come to the edge of a cliff, understand what I mean. How many times have you asked, "And then?" or "What comes next?" only to have the child look at you in confusion? Posting an extended number chart not only affords visual affirmation that there is life after 100—that we do, indeed, count beyond 100—but also demonstrates how the second century, so to speak, follows the same pattern as the first, and so on throughout our number system. This realization is often a powerful "Aha!" for many children.

The power of a number grid, however, extends beyond counting and patterns. At all elementary grade levels, it can serve as a tool for computation. Let's take a look at a second-grade class solving 53 + 32. The teacher, Mrs. Carreiro, had presented a word problem that set up adding these two numbers. She asked the students to solve the equation any way they wanted. Some solved it on paper using the U.S. historically taught algorithm; some solved it on paper using partial sums; others used base ten blocks, while others used the number line. A few used the 100 chart, among them, Emily, who was willing to share her solution:

Emily: I used the 100 chart and got 85.
Mrs. Carreiro: Would you come up to the chart and show how you used it?
Emily (moving to the front of the room): I started here at 53 (pointing) and I jumped down three rows and moved over two spaces and landed on 85.
Mrs. Carreiro: Why did you "jump down" three rows and then "move over" two spaces?
Emily: I was thinking that 32 is 3 tens and 2 ones.
Mrs. Carreiro: How did that help you?
Emily: Well, I know that 53 add 1 ten is right below it—63 (pointing).
Mrs. Carreiro: And . . . ?
Emily: So, ten more is 63, 2 tens more is 73, 3 tens more is 83, and then there are just the 2 ones left, so I just slide over two spots.

The 100 chart has given Emily the tool to solve this problem mentally while helping her keep track of where she is. Eventually, she'll get to the point where she'll internalize a mental model of the 100 number grid, which she will use with ease. As an adult, I walk around with both a number line and a number grid in my head and use them all the time to compute mentally (addition and subtraction). I started to do this as a student and continue to do it now because it allows me to "see" my thinking. I love it when I see students doing the same!

3. MANIPULATIVES COLLECTION

▶ *What*

Every elementary classroom benefits from having a collection of manipulatives and a specific area in which these assorted materials are housed, often in a section of the classroom known as the "math center." Wherever they are, to maximize their use, manipulatives must be accessible to students, which means that they should be in clearly marked, accessible and portable containers (see, for example, Figures 2.8 and 2.9). The assortment may include but is not limited to base ten blocks, calculators, counting chips and other assorted counters, clocks, coins, geoboards, 100 charts (laminated student size), measurement tools, pattern blocks, playing cards, scales with weights, tangrams, ten frames.

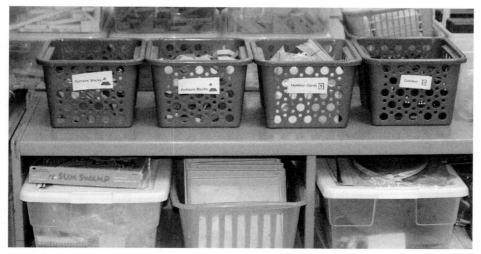

Figure 2.8: This second-grade manipulatives collection is made with "bargain" baskets and wooden planks and provides accessible and organized materials.

Figure 2.9: This twenty-cubby storage unit offers a great way to keep objects organized in this kindergarten classroom.

▶ Why

The purposes of a manipulatives collection are

- to provide students easy access to materials that will help them to see relationships, to make connections, and to deepen their conceptual understanding in concrete ways;
- to help students represent their reasoning as they prove their strategies in solving problems; and
- to foster independence in students to promote the belief that using such resources will foster their growth as problem solvers and mathematical thinkers.

▶ Where

The manipulatives collection can be stored anywhere in the room. It must be clean, organized, labeled, and accessible to all.

▶ *Magnification*

Because school budgets and teachers' personal budgets vary greatly around the country, the amount of money spent on manipulatives, support materials, and storage units in elementary classrooms varies widely. No matter your budget, however, materials must be accessible to students. A great way to accomplish accessibility is to display materials in see-through containers and have materials out in the open as much as possible. In addition, labels (words or diagrams) should be affixed to each container. I am always on the lookout for deals on containers. (My husband calls me "The Queen of Plastic" and I wear the crown proudly!) Regularly check your local dollar store for great deals; I am there so often that staff members know my name and often show me new items. If your classroom is not outfitted with wooden storage units with individual cubbies and color-coordinated bins, you can construct a manipulatives center out of wooden planks set on cement blocks, a low-cost, no-frills option. The aim is to have a place for students to gather objects that will help them "do" math while proving their answers and showing their thinking.

4. STUDENT WORK SAMPLES

▶ *What*

Samples of student work are just that—representative examples of the effort and thinking students have exhibited in mathematics, both as individuals and in a group. Such samples include a written solution to a problem complete with words, numbers, and diagrams; a journal entry; a mathematical biography; a three-dimensional representation of a solution to a problem; and a flowchart, survey, diorama, poster, or mobile, depicting, explaining, or elaborating on students' thoughts, feelings, opinions, and perceptions.

▶ *Why*

The purposes of posted student work are

- to make a clear statement about the importance of their work in mathematics,
- to serve as a source of pride for students in their completed work,
- to demonstrate multiple solutions to the same problem and sometimes even multiple correct solutions, and
- to provide a model for other students in mathematical communication, representation, and reasoning.

◗ *Where*

Student work can be placed on walls, on doors and windows, and on ceilings (as allowed by fire codes). Some classrooms have "math corners" where student work is displayed on bulletin boards, dividers, and tables. Many schools have display cases where exemplary work is celebrated—use them for math!

◗ *Magnification*

When I first started teaching, I worked feverishly to construct beautiful bulletin boards that made the room warm and inviting, or so I thought. I created most of the bulletin boards, although one displayed student artwork, one presented students' handwriting samples, and one showed monthly "creative writing" samples. Times have changed—as they should. Displays of student work are no longer primarily for completed projects that are for "show" purposes only. Let's look at Figure 2.10. Fourth-grade students worked together to build a fraction number line that extends from 0 to 3. Students were given index cards with one fraction or a mixed numeral on each and had to determine which goes where (denominators include halves, thirds, fourths, sixths, and eighths).

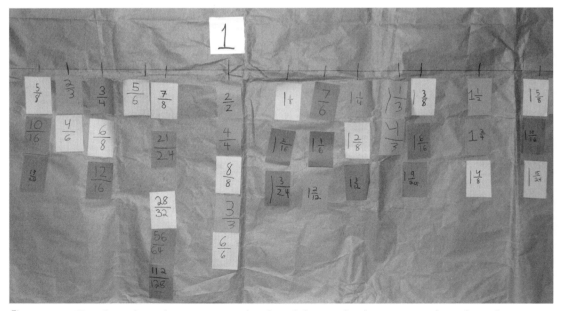

Figure 2.10: Fourth-grade students constructed and used this number line at points throughout the year.

They constructed the number line at the beginning of the unit on fractions and used it consistently within the unit as a reference tool to solve problems. One such problem included ordering the following from least to greatest: $1\frac{7}{8}$, $\frac{3}{4}$, $\frac{6}{5}$, $1\frac{1}{4}$, $\frac{4}{3}$, $\frac{2}{2}$.

Enrico: Maybe we should start with the greatest one first.

Simone: We could also start with the smallest one. I don't think it makes a difference.

Enrico: Fine. The smallest one is $\frac{3}{4}$, right? It's the only one that is less than one whole.

Simone: Right. And then $\frac{2}{2}$ is next because that's the same as a whole.

Enrico: Yup. Now it's tricky. $1\frac{1}{4}$ seems like the next one because it's just a little bit over 1 or is it $\frac{4}{3}$?

Simone: I'm not sure, but I think it might be $\frac{6}{5}$.

Enrico: Really? I don't think so; 6 out of 5 is more than 4 out of 3.

Simone: No. Look at the number line. $\frac{4}{3}$ is one whole plus one more third and is here (pointing on the number line). $\frac{6}{5}$ is one whole plus one more fifth and that's here on the number line (pointing)—to the left of where $\frac{4}{3}$ is. And look—$1\frac{1}{4}$ would be right between the two of them!

Enrico: That's cool. I get it! That means the largest one is $1\frac{7}{8}$ because that's way closer to 2 on the number line.

This exhibit of student work served so many purposes. The constructed number line first helped students think and puzzle about the order of numbers. It then served as a tool for solving problems and justifying their thinking. It also represented the collaboration and cooperation students engaged in to get the job done, thereby allowing them to share a collective pride in their accomplishment. The teacher kept the number line up for the length of the unit and then removed it from the wall. Later in the year, however, she put it back up when the class began a unit on decimals, which were added to the number line. What a great way to help students use what they know to make connections!

Now take a look at the photo *Name That Plant* (Figure 2.11).

The children were told that they would be "planting" the idea that numbers can be represented in multiple ways—that they could select a number and present it any way they chose. At first glance, this approach may not appear to have a strong mathematical purpose, however, it illustrates what goes on in that first-grade classroom. This is a task that is open to all students and has multiple entry points.

As you can see, there is a range in the size of the numbers from 18 to 9,995, as well as a range in the types of representations, including counting

Figure 2.11: "Name That Plant" bulletin board in first-grade classroom

sequences, tallies, coins, base ten block models, and assorted number combinations. In the close-up of the "18" plant, the student drew a regular hexagon and labeled each of the sides with a "3" to show a total perimeter of 18. Although this student did not yet have facility with large numbers, he had a solid understanding of some very important basics: that perimeter is the distance around the outside of a figure, that regular hexagons have sides of equal length, and that labeling a figure is a good practice and a helpful strategy. It may be hard to tell by looking at students' work, but the teacher got a lot of mileage from it, as she referred to it during a lesson using pattern blocks. As she led a discussion on the attributes of the blocks, she asked the students to "look over at Jessie's number plant for 18. What do you notice about the sides of the hexagon?" She also observed students accessing it when they were doing "number of the day" activities:

Celia: Look at what Yoshika did for her 177 plant. She used part/part/whole and did a pattern. I'm going to do that for "Today's Number."
Danielle: What do you mean?
Celia: She did 100 + 77 and 90 + 87. So for today, Day 142, I'm going to do 100 + 42, 90 + 52, 80 + 62.

Danielle: I'm going to use plus 0 like Joe did and then minus 0 and then plus and minus 10 and 20. That's a pattern, too!

It thrills me when I walk into classrooms and see vibrant displays of student work that serve multiple purposes. They certainly add a great deal to the landscape, creating a warm and inviting classroom, but they do so much more. Displays of student work are both teaching and learning tools that are *of* the children, *by* the children, and *for* the children!

5. DAILY SCHEDULE

◗ *What*

A daily schedule gives the beginning and ending time for each segment of the day. The day of the week and the date should both appear above the schedule, written in various formats (Figure 2.12). In K–2 classrooms, clock faces often appear next to each entry (Figure 2.13).

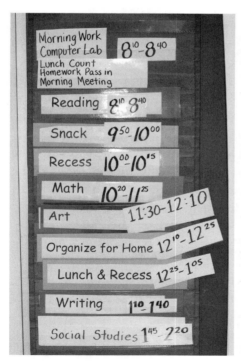

Figure 2.12: A daily schedule without clock faces in third-grade classroom

Figure 2.13: A daily schedule with clock faces in second-grade classroom

▶ *Why*

The purposes of a daily schedule are

- to provide an overview of the day for the students, so that they can see how time can be organized and planned;
- to help students make the connection between the passage of time and the telling of time; and
- to give students a model for having flexibility within planning, as is often the case in everyday elementary classroom life.

▶ *Where*

Visibility of the schedule is key. Position the schedule where students gather for whole-class instruction. It can be in a corner of the whiteboard, on a poster-sized sticky note, or on an easel—whatever works for you and your physical layout.

▶ *Magnification*

Are you a list person? Do you make lists of all that you have to do in a day, anticipating some things on the list, not so much for others? Do you have a sense of accomplishment when you check off something on your list? I have to answer a resounding, "Yes!" A daily schedule in a classroom is a good idea. There is something reassuring about the presence of a daily schedule displayed on the board or a chart stand. It sends the message that a purposeful day is planned. In the younger grades, when symbols accompany the words to indicate the activity, all children understand the sequence of the day. Many students look forward to some parts of the day and plan accordingly. Having the start and end times for each "period" reassures students; they can check where they are in the scope of the activity and of the day. Clocks that indicate start times can help those who are learning how to tell time.

A posted schedule aids in both teaching how to tell time and computing elapsed time in the real-life context of the school day. In addition, a posted schedule provides opportunities to model how often schedules need to be modified, which highlights both the teacher's and the students' flexibility. What a great life lesson for students. If an unexpected school assembly, fire drill, or extended reading lesson upsets the original schedule, they see how to adapt, adjust, and move on through the day.

6. DESIGNATED MATHEMATICS CENTER/AREA

◗ *What*

It seems as if every elementary classroom has a reading corner. This is a critical and essential component. In addition, a math corner, or math area, a place designated for doing, thinking of, and reading mathematics is a great idea. Manipulatives, math literature collections, and math games might be found in this area. Tables, chairs, pillows, and whiteboards are other possible items found here.

◗ *Why*

The purposes of a designated mathematics area are

- to highlight for students the message that mathematics is important in the elementary classroom,
- to give students a sense of ownership of all things mathematical in their room, and
- to underscore that students have myriad resources that can be accessed at any time to support their mathematical work.

◗ *Where*

The designated mathematics area should be in the place in your classroom where it fits the best: in a corner or in the center of the room. It is optimal to have all of the components of the center in one place; avoid, for example, putting some manipulatives in one corner of the room and others in a separate place.

◗ *Magnification*

When I walk into my small-town public library, there is a corner room off to the side that has big, comfy leather chairs with ottomans here and there, soft lighting, and beautiful pictures. I want to stop and nestle in for as long as I can because the warmth and invitation are palpable. Many of you probably have recreated such a place for reading in your classrooms, perhaps not with leather chairs and ottomans but equally attractive. A math corner, or area, can be that, too. Figure 2.14 depicts some of the attractive features of a math area. You can see why students are drawn to this place. It houses the manipulatives

Figure 2.14: The math center in Tina Adamson's kindergarten classroom houses manipulatives, games, and other resources. Whole-class and small-group lessons as well as partner work take place here.

collection on the perimeter, making it a convenient place to work with materials. There are clipboards, pencils, and calculators as well as student-sized whiteboards and one large whiteboard all students can use. Students can sit on a rug as they work together. They can also sit on carpet squares. There is a small game table in one corner bordered on the other side by a collection of fiction and nonfiction "math" books. A rocking chair and pillows add another dimension. This area has been built with the express purpose of welcoming mathematical thinkers. It's as if there is a neon sign blinking "Mathematical Thinkers Welcome!"

7. MATHEMATICS WORD WALL

◆ *What*

A staple of every elementary classroom is "the word wall," a core group of reading words pertinent to the grade level. The mathematics word wall, though less common, is no less critical. It is a collection of the math words, terms, and phrases highlighted throughout the year in your classroom. For each word wall entry, include a definition, a picture, a diagram or a visual representation (see Figures 2.15 and 2.16). Make sure these are large enough to be seen from a distance.

Figure 2.15: Two fourth graders consult the student-constructed math word wall.

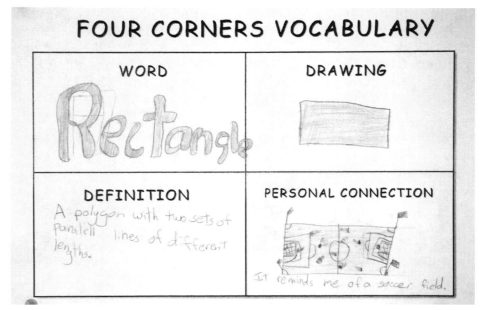

Figure 2.16: Word wall card, up close and personal

◗ *Why*

The purposes of a mathematics word wall are

- to showcase core mathematical words, terms, and phrases;
- to furnish another resource for explanation and review of key terms;
- to signal the relevance and importance of precise and meaningful mathematical vocabulary; and
- to heighten the sense of the classroom as a community of shared learning.

◗ *Where*

As with the designated mathematics center, the mathematics word wall should be placed where it fits best in your classroom. Estimate the amount of space you will need for about 25 to 30 core words, terms, and phrases.

◗ *Magnification*

Premade word walls for reading, writing, and even mathematics are available. Although these may be convenient and easier to post, it's best to view the wall as a "working" mathematics word wall. That's an explicit distinction because it indicates that the word wall requires student involvement. Students can make the word wall cards themselves and introduce each one to the class as it is added to the wall. The value-added dimension of student ownership is worth the expenditure of time and energy. It is more powerful that the wall be viewed as a work in progress, with words added throughout the school year. In addition, word wall cards serve as reference points to aid in daily work and to reinforce concepts and terminology that refine and extend understanding.

Let's take a look at two third graders working together to solve a problem that requires finding the perimeter of a figure.

Amy: Okay, we need to figure out the perimeter of this shape. (She points to the diagram on the workbook page on geodot paper.)

David: Let's make the shape on the geoboard. (They copy the shape onto the geoboard, being careful to check to make sure it is the same.)

Amy: So the perimeter is 13. (She counts the squares on the interior of the shape.)

David: No, that's not right. You counted the inside—that's not how to get the perimeter.

Amy: Yes, it is. You just need to count what's covered inside.

David: No. Look. (He points to and then reads the card on the word wall for *perimeter*.) Perimeter means you *parade* around the outside of the thing and count the steps you take like it shows here.

Amy: I keep getting area and perimeter mixed up. (Together they count the "steps" they take as they move around the outside of the shape.) Oh, it's 16, not 13! That's different.

8. MATHEMATICS LITERATURE COLLECTION

▶ *What*

This collection should include nonfiction and fiction grade-level selections, some above and some below level (see an example in Figure 2.17). Commercially available kits can be purchased in addition to gathering books on your own. Remember that picture books are appropriate for all grade levels and offer an easy way to "pull" students into mathematical thinking.

Figure 2.17: Mathematics literature collection

▶ *Why*

The purposes of a mathematics literature collection are

- to extend the mathematics being taught,
- to draw attention to how mathematics connects to the everyday world, and
- to engage students more fully in the fun and wonder of mathematics.

◗ *Where*

The mathematics literature collection should be placed within the designated mathematics center, or area. Books can be sorted according to topics, author, and purpose.

◗ *Magnification*

I am back in my library again, and I am heading to my favorite section—mystery/suspense books and CDs. I always approach with a sense of excitement, as I know I am going to find something that entices me and brings me joy. Students experience similar joy in the classroom as they are drawn to a mathematics literature collection. It is a beautiful thing to see!

Classroom collections vary, of course, in part due to financial considerations. While some classrooms have an ample collection of books supplied by the school, the teacher, or parents, not every classroom is as fortunate. This does not mean, however, that a classroom has to go without a mathematics literature collection. The school and the public library can be great resources. Students can bring in their own books to lend to the classroom collection. Book lists abound in both hard copy and online and can provide you with grade-level-appropriate titles. Among helpful online sources is http://www.cde.ca.gov/ci/sc/ll/ from the California Department of Education. It lists both mathematics and science literature, searchable by topic, grade level, and standards. Further, most programs provide a suggested list of mathematics literature—*Everyday Mathematics; Investigations in Number, Data, and Space*; and *Think Math*, among them—so take advantage of these even if you are not using these programs. Include both nonfiction and fiction selections, and capitalize on the wonderful array of picture books at all grade levels. Go with your instincts and include less obvious books. *The Grapes of Math* (Tang 2001) is a popular choice; so, too, is *Market Day* (Bunting 1996), a less obvious one. Eve Bunting's description of the once-a-month market day in the small Irish village of her childhood is bursting with math potential: from the total number of pigs, cows, and goats to the number of feet seen in an illustration, from the amount of money spent on certain items to the total cost of a week's worth of goods; the possibilities are endless!

9. TECHNOLOGY

▶ *What*

Access to technology depends on your school district's ability to provide classrooms with current tools for the twenty-first century. At one end of the spectrum are interactive whiteboards (Figure 2.18) and document cameras, both of which are phenomenal instructional tools. Computers (Figure 2.19), especially laptops, enhance classroom experiences. Less cutting edge, yet still useful, is the overhead projector. Calculators still have an important place in the elementary classroom.

Figure 2.18: Hussain explains his strategy on the interactive board to his second-grade classmates.

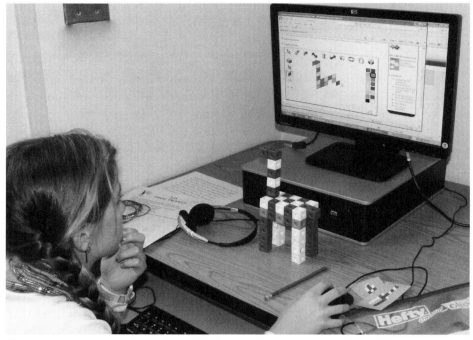

Figure 2.19: Fourth-grader Chloe is completing a two-dimensional representation and directions for others to make the "cube toy" that she created.

▶ *Why*

The purposes of technology are

- to capitalize on the interactive nature of learning,
- to facilitate sharing student thinking,
- to increase opportunities for students to check their own work,
- to provide opportunities for students to engage more completely, and
- to underscore technological proficiency as a twenty-first-century need.

▶ *Where*

The placement of technology obviously depends on what you have available. Some teachers have a computer corner, or stations, while others have access to laptop carts. Calculators can be at every student's desk, in a collection for groups or pods of desks, or stored with the manipulatives (although this is not preferable if this is the only place calculators are present in the classroom).

◗ *Magnification*

This is another area in which the range is large, as there are classrooms that have a wealth of technology with everything, from the newest calculators for every student to multiple laptops and interactive whiteboards. Again, the presence of "things" does not make a classroom vibrate with mathematical learning. As you know, it is *how* these tools are used that can make a difference. The effective use of something as simple as an overhead projector can work wonders if a teacher uses it along with manipulatives so that students can "see" the concept in a concrete way. Further, students can share their solutions to problems on an overhead projector so that others can closely follow their thinking. For classrooms with more advanced technology, interactive whiteboards can pull up virtual manipulatives to support the development of a concept.

In addition, access to the Internet through these interactive boards links students to interactive games and activities that further support a lesson's goals. A document camera, a tool somewhere between an overhead projector and an interactive whiteboard, enables a student to position his work under the lens, projecting the image for all to see—no muss, no fuss, no bored students waiting their turn to recreate their work (as with an overhead). Group dialogue can begin on the spot.

10. MULTIPLE INSTRUCTIONAL SETTINGS

◗ What

This is all about organizing your classroom with multiple places for students to gather for instruction and to work on mathematics. Further, students should be able to move among these settings with ease and fluidity. See examples in Figures 2.20–2.22.

◗ Why

The purposes of multiple instructional settings are

- to provide optimal settings for directed lessons to the whole class, targeted focus lessons to small groups, collaborative work with partners, and individually geared and paced opportunities;
- to give students ample opportunities to work to their strengths and to improve their skills in various work modes; and
- to signal that learning takes place in a variety of settings.

Figure 2.20: Monica Matthews conducts a whole-class mini-lesson in fourth grade.

Figure 2.21: This small group of kindergarten students is working on story problems with teacher Stephany Woodward.

Figure 2.22: Claire Nicholson is checking in on a third-grade student working independently.

◗ *Where*

You gain a great deal by setting up your classroom with multiple purposes in mind for different instructional settings. These include a whole-class setting with students seated so that they can see the whiteboard, chalkboard, inter-active whiteboard, or document camera. If possible, have a table designated for small-group instruction (kidney-shaped tables are ideal for this) that can accommodate four to six students and the teacher. In addition, places where students can work in pairs or individually—at desks or at small tables or sitting on carpet squares or pillows—create a comfortable environment for learning.

Do not hesitate to make changes as the year progresses (or as a colleague with a new eye to your room may suggest). Something that looks good initially may not play out as well as anticipated, or a new inspiration may maximize your physical space.

▶ *Magnification*

When you first walk into Mr. Solomon's fifth-grade classroom, you notice that the central meeting area on a rug is at the back of the room. The rug is bordered by a whiteboard on one side with a chart stand and an overhead projector to the left. Two long two-tiered shelving units are opposite each other on which bins of math materials, student work folders, and math games are stored. The fourth side of the rug is open to the rest of the room on the side opposite the whiteboard. This is where Mr. Solomon holds his opening mini-lesson for the whole class and often has lesson closure as well. In addition, this space is also used for breakout small groups or partner work. At the front of the room is a rectangular table (8 feet by $2\frac{1}{2}$ feet) with a whiteboard behind it; Mr. Solomon often gathers small groups of students here for directed lessons. Students can access a bank of four computers along the side of another wall for reinforcement and extension. Twenty-five desks are arranged in six pods (five groups of four desks and one group of five desks). A math center occupies a corner opposite the rug that includes a smaller area rug, a rocking chair, several pillows, and a bookcase filled with math games and bins of books labeled by topic. Off to the side is another round table for student use. By thoughtfully arranging his room, Mr. Solomon has created multiple, flexible instructional settings.

Picture this: now you are entering a fourth-grade classroom—not your own—for the first time. It is October, and as you take your first step inside, you stop for a moment and look. Most likely you notice where the students are, what they are doing and saying, where the teacher is and what she is saying. Now let's widen the scope to take a look at the physical plant—the landscape of the classroom. Can you find a number line, a 100 chart, manipulatives all accessible to the students? Can you see student work samples and a daily schedule? Is there a designated math center that beckons to students and a mathematics word wall that is a work in progress? What about a mathematics literature collection? Is it there? Do you see technology and evidence of its use? Do you see multiple instructional settings? Are there places for individual, partner, small-group, and whole-class work?

Time for that caveat again: You know, I know, everyone knows that the simple presence of these components does not ensure that good things are happening either with them or because of them. The bottom line is these components only matter when they are used appropriately, strategically, and consistently. If they are absent, however, then they cannot be used at all; for that reason, it is important to note them as critical elements of mathematics teaching and learning that should be visible in the classroom landscape.

Paraphrasing the Samuel Johnson quote at the start of the chapter, it is easy to see that, while making changes takes effort, when the advantages of doing so are magnified, the reasons for our efforts are more powerful. It is time now to move our scope to another aspect of the "look" of a classroom—the look of the lesson to see what additional advantages can be magnified. Pause for a moment and think about what you would like to see in your classroom and what you would like others to see you doing as you work to provide effective instruction.

CHAPTER 3

THE LOOK OF THE LESSON: TEACHERS

What we see depends mainly on what we look for.
—John Lubbock, English biologist and politician

Let's sharpen the mental image of what you might see yourself doing during a lesson and magnify some techniques that lead to effective instruction. Let's explore the *what, why,* and *when* of these important elements, as each plays a part in strong mathematics teaching. As in the previous chapter, a caveat here: these are not the only significant components; they are, rather, a starting place for our collective thinking and reflection. They include the following:

1. Differentiating instruction
2. Checking for understanding
3. Facilitating mathematical thinking

4.   Identifying student misconceptions
5.   Providing written feedback
6.   Using wait time
7.   Setting and sharing lesson goals/objectives

Before we begin, let me acknowledge that the first two components—
differentiating instruction and checking for understanding—are so important that entire books have been devoted to them. Why, then, include them
in such an abbreviated way? The simple answer is that, whenever I think of
good mathematics teaching, these components are at the core. As a beginning and experienced classroom teacher, I have constantly worked to
improve and to refine my practice of each. As a mathematics specialist and
building principal, I worked to help teachers improve and refine their practice in these areas. As a consultant and coach, I continue to improve and
refine my own and other teachers' practice of these components. I have chosen to include them to serve as a reminder to experienced teachers to continue to be aware of and to reflect on their practice of these components and
as an invitation to beginning teachers to delve more deeply and understand
more fully the potential impact of each.

1. DIFFERENTIATING INSTRUCTION

▶ *What*

While most of us agree with the concept of differentiated instruction, it can
be overwhelming and even impossible to put into practice. Differentiated
instruction is doable, manageable, and attainable, but it takes time and
effort. As a beginning teacher, I thought differentiated instruction meant
individualized instruction. This is when I had (only) sixteen fifth and sixth
graders in my math class, all performing below grade level, and I scrambled
every night to create a unique "math menu" for each student for the next
day, geared to what I believed were their individual needs. I did not see until
years later that, even though each student was learning to some degree, by
individualizing in this way, I was depriving my students of learning from
their peers, collaborating with their classmates, and sharing their thinking
with people other than me. At the same time, I was putting unreasonable
pressure on myself in my well-intentioned efforts to meet every student
where he was, move him along at his own pace, match his learning style,
deepen his conceptual understanding, and improve his procedural skills.

RECOMMENDED RESOURCES

Leading and Managing a Differentiated Classroom (Tomlinson and Imbeau 2010)
Tomlinson and her colleague, Marcia Imbeau, offer a manageable description of what is at the heart of differentiated instruction, "the modification of four curriculum-related elements—content, process, product, and affect—which are based on three categories of student need and variance—readiness, interest, and learning profile" (15). The book is an invaluable resource on differentiation across all content areas.

Math for All: Differentiating Instruction, Grades K–2 (Dacey and Salemi 2007) and *Grades 3–5* (Dacey and Lynch 2007)
The first two books in this three-book series provide a substantive overview of the elementary grades K–5 in an insightful and accessible manner—it's a great series to have on your professional bookshelf. Dacey and Lynch offer ways to differentiate both within a unit and within a lesson while providing support in creating and modifying tasks to meet the diverse needs of your students as well as giving techniques to manage it all. (See the third book in the series authored by Dacey and Gartland for grades six to eight.)

After I taught kindergarten and while I was teaching third grade, I began to see how differentiating instruction means something different. I developed my own working, if simplistic, definition. I saw differentiated instruction as looking at a lesson, analyzing the objectives, and then modifying what I was asking students to accomplish and how they could demonstrate that they had met the goals. I based this on where I knew (or thought I knew) them to be—at grade level, below grade level, above grade level in terms of that concept or skill. This approach allowed me to differentiate to a greater degree, ultimately serving my students better.

I wish I'd had the resources then that are currently available to help establish, maintain, refine, and improve your ability to differentiate instruction. I suggest starting with or revisiting the work of Carol Ann Tomlinson, a recognized leader in this field. For a more targeted focus on mathematics, see the work of Linda Dacey and Jayne Lynch for important and practical suggestions (see Recommended Resources).

For the purposes of this book, let's use the general frame offered by Tomlinson, apply it to mathematics, and examine instruction and the instructional modifications teachers make:

- Content—the knowledge, understanding, and skills we want students to learn
- Process—how students come to understand or make sense of the content

- Product—how students demonstrate what they have come to know, understand, and are able to do after an extended period of learning
- Affect—how students' emotions and feelings impact their learning (Tomlinson and Imbeau 2010, 15–16)

▶ Why

The purposes of differentiating instruction are

- to meet the needs of students in learning mathematical content;
- to meet the needs of students in terms of learning styles and preferences;
- to establish a positive, respectful, and motivational learning environment that blends both the cognitive and affective dimensions of learning; and
- to optimize the learning potential of all students.

▶ When

Just about every lesson can be tweaked and most likely needs to be tweaked in some way to meet the content, process, product, or affect needs of your students in a more precise and focused manner.

▶ *Magnification*

Let's look at an example of how to differentiate a lesson that involves problem solving, which is at the crux of many mathematics programs. Some districts and schools are committed to teaching the same eight to ten problem-solving strategies throughout the grades—making a list, drawing a picture, making a table, working backward, and so forth. Many schools have purchased problem-solving print materials, with strategies geared for each grade level.

On a Thursday morning in October, Mrs. Benson, a third-grade teacher in a school that had purchased problem-solving materials, had just finished a whole-class lesson and had modeled how making a table to organize information was a possible strategy that could be used to solve a particular problem. She then set the students to work on solving problems with partners. The problem sets the teacher distributed, however, were not the same: most students were given third-grade problems to solve, some were given second-grade problems, some received fourth-grade problems, and two partner pairs received fifth-grade problem sets. All students received the same general instruction by the teacher, "We made a table to solve our problem together today—another problem-solving strategy we are adding to our growing collection of strategies. You may decide to use that strategy as you work with your partners right now, or you may choose another strategy you think will work as well or better."

Mrs. Benson then distributed the various problem sets to the students. All of the problems were finding the "mystery" numbers of coins based on a set of conditions (see Figures 3.1–3.3).

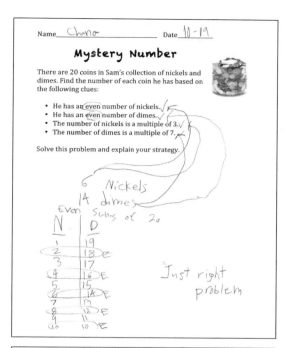

Figure 3.1:
Grade-level problem

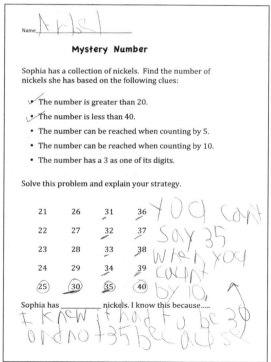

Figure 3.2: A bit of scaffolding helps students get started on this problem.

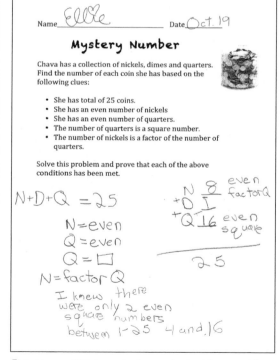

Figure 3.3: Ellie's work shows she is able to tackle a more challenging "mystery number" problem.

The first problem is geared to the third-grade level, the second to the second-grade level, and the third to the fourth-grade level. The content differentiation involves the number of coins and the vocabulary usage and application. The process and product differentiation lie in the number and type of conditions set to find the mystery numbers, in the scaffolding (or not) of the presence of an organizing table, in the level of explanation needed, and in the generation of a similar problem. All students were asked to assess the level of difficulty.

Granted, this is not the only way to differentiate, yet it is effective in teaching problem-solving strategies. While the students in the class all needed to extend their table-making skills, they were ready to do so with problems of varying complexity, based on their performance levels.

2. CHECKING FOR UNDERSTANDING

◆ *What*

Checking for understanding has always been a part of strong teaching and has received even greater attention since being identified by Saphier, Haley-Speca, and Gower (see Recommended Resource). Figure 3.4 provides an example.

Saphier and his coauthors define checking for understanding relatively simply as a group of actions seen "when teachers are trying to determine whether students are confused" (2008, 190). One of their four levels of

Figure 3.4: Second-grade students respond to their teacher's check for understanding.

RECOMMENDED RESOURCE

The Skillful Teacher (Saphier, Haley-Speca, and Gower 2008)
Generally considered a staple in both preservice and inservice professional development courses, this is well worth having as a resource. The authors synthesize best practice and theory and offer practical suggestions in eighteen areas to improve teaching skills.

---

checking for understanding is reading aspects of students' body language, such as facial expressions and body postures that may signal confusion. Teachers often stop instruction to engage in more direct checking, which entails asking various questions. Another method of checking for understanding, first identified by Madeline Hunter (1982), is *dipsticking* in which the teacher asks students to self-assess and give a physical symbol (thumbs up, down, or sideways; head nod; hand on head; unison responses, etc.). These actions can be integrated into your lessons in addition to using color-coded signals (red—Help!; green—Good to go; yellow—Quick question) with cards, cube towers, or plastic cups. To individualize and give more personal feedback, ask students to write their answers to a question on a personal-sized whiteboard (or paper on a clipboard) to be raised toward you as you check for understanding.

▶ Why

The purposes of checking for understanding are

- to determine the level of students' understanding—what they understand,
- to identify at what point(s) understanding is not present—when they don't understand, and
- to provide opportunities to modify instruction and clarify understanding.

▶ When

When checking for understanding is incorporated at all points during mathematics instruction, you are better able to maximize student learning. These "checking" actions are beneficial when you introduce new concepts, terms, and procedures, as well as when you make connections and give directions.

▶ *Magnification*

Consider how this teacher uses a few methods of checking for understanding in this fourth-grade lesson on classifying shapes in which students have small whiteboards:

Mr. Gates: On your whiteboard, please draw a quadrilateral. (He gives time for the task to be completed.) Now raise your boards so I can see them. (He does a quick scan and notes that all have drawn some form of a quadrilateral.) Now draw a quadrilateral that has at least one pair of parallel opposite sides and is *not* a rectangle. If you understand what you are being asked to do and know how to get started, give a thumb's up signal. (He notes that one student has a sideways thumb and one has a thumbs down; he quickly clarifies the directions for them and waits until all have drawn something.) Please hold up your boards so I can see. (He scans the boards, notes the responses, and continues by calling on students at various levels of understanding.)

Mr. Gates now knows that most students seem to have a workable understanding of some of the attributes of a quadrilateral because they all had drawn a closed shape with four sides. He also has an idea that the second requirement of the task (not a rectangle) seemed to present a problem for four students, all of whom drew a square. Mr. Gates now has to tease out the basis for the students' incorrect answers. He sets the rest of the class to work on a game of attributes, while he calls the four students to the rug so that he can work with them.

3. FACILITATING MATHEMATICAL THINKING

▶ *What*

An essential part of being a teacher is to model what it means to be a mathematical thinker and then facilitate such thinking in students (Figure 3.5). To that end, you can develop, sculpt, set an example, establish a paradigm, furnish a pattern, provide an exemplar, and present a prototype of the

- use of manipulatives to introduce a concept or to explain mathematical thinking;
- application of a problem-solving heuristic. George Polya's four-step process is a strong one (see Recommended Resource on page 42):

- ◆ Understand the problem (Read to find what you are being asked to find or show.)
- ◆ Devise a plan (Choose a strategy—or two.)
- ◆ Carry out the plan (Do it! Follow your plan.)
- ◆ Look back (Does the answer make sense? What worked? What didn't?)
- use of mathematical notation;
- purpose of writing in mathematics;
- use of mathematical vocabulary;
- integration of technology;
- importance of perseverance; and
- gains to be made from mistakes.

Figure 3.5: Fourth-grade teacher Jaime Miller facilitates the mathematical thinking of her students.

◗ Why

The purposes of facilitating mathematical thinking are

- to foster deeper understanding,
- to support the development of precision and clarity, and
- to demonstrate that thinking is valued.

RECOMMENDED RESOURCE

How to Solve It (Polya 1945)
As a young man in Budapest, George Polya found that, while he was not good at memorizing information in mathematics, he was good at solving problems. He created a series of steps to help others solve problems and shared his method with countless elementary and secondary teachers while teaching at Brown and Stanford universities. This oldie but goodie has stood the test of time.

◆ *When*

Optimize "teachable moments" throughout the day.

◆ *Magnification*

This is part of a fifth-grade lesson on what multiplying fractions really means. Ms. Lin is with a group of four students at a kidney-shaped table in the back of the room.

Ms. Lin: Let's work on proving that one-half of one-third is one-sixth. (She writes that on the whiteboard behind her.) Can someone write that as a number sentence and explain? (Hands go up.) Julio?

Julio: (As he writes, he explains.) It's the same as $\frac{1}{2} \times \frac{1}{3} = \frac{1}{6}$ because "of" means to multiply.

Ms. Lin: That's right. Let me ask about how we can now *prove* that to be correct with pattern blocks. Any thoughts? (She waits but gets no response.) Okay, let's start with the statement that the hexagon (holding one up) is equal to one whole. Any thoughts from there?

Serena: Well, then the trapezoid is $\frac{1}{2}$, and the diamond is $\frac{1}{3}$.

Ms. Lin: Correct. The trapezoid is $\frac{1}{2}$ and the blue *rhombus* is $\frac{1}{3}$. What about the triangle?

Miguel: That's easy. $\frac{1}{6}$.

Ms. Lin: How do you know?

Miguel: Because it takes 6 triangles to cover a hexagon.

Ms. Lin: Great. Now everyone get a blue rhombus in front of you and tell the value. (They all do.) $\frac{1}{3}$. Now looking at this rhombus, what is one-half of it?

All: A triangle!

Ms. Lin: So let me hear it in words first.

Julio: The triangle is one-half of the rhombus.

Ms. Lin: Yes . . . and . . . ?

Julio: And the rhombus is one-third of the hexagon whole.

Ms. Lin: True. Number sentence?

Alana: I think it would be $\frac{1}{2} \times \frac{1}{3} = \frac{1}{6}$.

Ms. Lin: What do you notice?

Alana: That's what we started with. That's what you wanted us to prove!

As you can see, Ms. Lin modeled how to use a manipulative to prove a mathematical idea, how to approach a problem in steps by connecting to something previously learned, how to work the connection between words and numbers, how to use appropriate vocabulary, and how to use mathematical notation! Ms. Lin provided additional experience with this concept in center activities, allowing students to solidify and deepen their understanding while also giving her the chance to find out who "got it" and who needed more time with this mathematical idea.

4. IDENTIFYING STUDENT MISCONCEPTIONS

◆ *What*

Identifying student misconceptions is an important part of what teachers do in the classroom (see Figure 3.6). *Misconception* here means a misunderstanding that often leads to an erroneous idea or answer. Early on, many students, for example, internalize the idea that multiplication always results

Figure 3.6: With his teacher's help, Paul's misconception is identified.

in a larger number than the two numbers being multiplied. Students have a difficult time undoing this common misconception when they are multiplying with decimals and fractions.

Having the student explain her thinking with words, diagrams, numbers, or manipulatives, recording the student's thinking in its entirety as she explains it, and then following up with clarifying questions helps tease out the root of the student's misconception. This, of course, takes time, but the trade-off is worth it if it corrects the misconception.

◗ Why

The purposes of identifying student misconceptions are

- to provide in-the-moment information (formative) that allows for modification of instruction,
- to allow students an opportunity to clarify their thinking, and
- to prevent students from learning and practicing something that is incorrect.

◗ When

We must always be ready to identify student misconceptions when they happen during the lesson and perhaps even more important, before they happen. Take some time before a lesson to consider what the pitfalls might be. What are the possible misconceptions that students might already have? What are some new ones this topic might generate? You may choose to address them at various times, depending on how widespread they are. If a misconception is part of a whole-class lesson, you can unpack it at that moment if it appears that many of the students have the same misunderstanding. If it affects just a few of the students, you may want to signal that you will be calling a small group together immediately following the whole-group lesson. If you determine that it is one student, you may wish to dissect the misconception in an individual setting.

◗ *Magnification*

How you identify student misconceptions is tightly woven into content knowledge, as is knowing what to do when you uncover those misconceptions. A full discussion moves beyond the scope of this book, but there are several good resources to access (see Recommended Resources).

RECOMMENDED RESOURCES

Math Misconceptions, Pre-K–Grade 5: From Misunderstanding to Deep Understanding
(Bamberger, Oberdorf, and Schultz-Ferrell 2010)
The authors identify the most common student misconceptions, discuss the sources of these misunderstandings, and then provide strategies for helping both to avoid and to address them.

Zeroing in on Number and Operations: Key Ideas and Common Misconceptions, Grades Pre-K–8 (Dacey and Collins 2010/2011)
This grade-level series is rich with specific ideas and strategies for teaching core concepts and skills while addressing the misconceptions that often accompany them.

Let's take a look at Mrs. Rahman's second-grade classroom where the students had been working on various ways to find the difference between two 2-digit numbers, with partial differences as one of the algorithms. As she walked around the room checking students' work, Mrs. Rahman came across Paul who had completed both problems incorrectly, having written

$$
\begin{array}{rl}
47 & \\
\underline{-25} & \\
20 & (40 - 20) \\
\underline{-2} & (7 - 5) \\
18 & (20 - 2)
\end{array}
$$

Paul had solved the second problem in the same manner:

$$
\begin{array}{rl}
64 & \\
\underline{-33} & \\
30 & (60 - 30) \\
\underline{-1} & (4 - 3) \\
29 & (30 - 1)
\end{array}
$$

Mrs. Rahman had an idea that Paul had applied what he had learned about finding partial sums to finding partial differences, which worked up to a point. She sat down next to him and prompted him for his explanation:

Paul: I found the difference in the tens first, and I know that 40 take away 20 is 20. (He points to where he had written that.) Then I know that 7 minus 5 is 2. Then I put the two minuses together and get 18.

Mrs. Rahman: I see how you found the difference between the tens and the difference between the ones and got 20 and 2. How did you get 18?

Paul: 20 take away 2 is 18.

Mrs. Rahman: Why did you take 2 away from 20?

Paul: Because this is a take-away problem. If it was an add problem, I would add 20 and 2.

This confirmed for Mrs. Rahman that Paul was operating under the assumption that because you *add* the partial sums together to find the total sum, then by following that logic, you should *subtract* the partial differences to determine the total difference. She had found the root of his misconception and then worked with him with base ten blocks to help him rethink and then solidify his process correctly. Mrs. Rahman had Paul show 47 with base ten blocks (he counted out four 10s and seven 1s). Keeping with the take-away model of subtraction that Paul had used, she asked him to take away 20, which he did. She then asked him to take away 5, so he removed five 1s. When she asked him what he had left, he correctly stated that he had 22 left. Mrs. Rahman asked him how this was different from his first answer of 18. Paul was puzzled for a moment and then the light went on:

Paul: Oh. I get it! When I first did it, I took the 2 away from the 20. I'm not supposed to do that. I already took the ones away when I took five 1s from the seven 1s. The 2 is really showing what I had *left* for 1s and so that needs to be *added* to the 20 I have from the 10s stuff.

5. PROVIDING WRITTEN FEEDBACK

◆ What

As you know, feedback can be used in a descriptive (formative) way as well as in an evaluative (summative) way. On written student work, feedback can be seen in

- short comments written in the margins,
- longer comments written on a cover page, and
- checkmarks and comments on a rubric.

As with other elements of strong teaching, remember these points about feedback. Feedback should be

- specific ("good thinking" is not enough. What about the thinking is good?),
- productive (giving students direction on where to go from where they are), and
- respectful (criticism can close students down).

Examples of "starting" phrases that meet these criteria include the following:

You're moving in the right direction. Can you add more to . . .
It's clear you took a risk when you . . .
Have you thought about making a connection between . . .
The first part of your thinking is clear; could you give more details about . . .

▶ Why

The purposes of providing written feedback to students are

- to let students know what they have done well,
- to let students know what their next steps might be,
- to provide a public forum for student mathematical thinking, and
- to increase motivation.

▶ When

Do not set unrealistic expectations for yourself. You do not need to give written feedback to every student every day. Incorporate an element of practicality and acknowledge that every once in a while you give a task that may not need a comment. On most posted student work, usually of a more summative nature, however, it is a good idea to make the written feedback visible. There should be further written feedback on student work—that may not be posted—at least three times per week.

RECOMMENDED RESOURCE

How to Give Effective Feedback to Your Students (Brookhart 2008)
The author provides an exemplary framework to help guide the giving of feedback, both in written and oral forms.

◆ *Magnification*

In Figure 3.7, you can see what the teacher wrote on this fourth grader's work. She provided affirmation of the quality of the student's work—"Excellent!"—something all students like to see. The teacher went further, however, by explaining what made the work excellent: "The explanation of your thinking was clear and concise and provided proof you know how to decompose numbers to multiply!"

Figure 3.7:
The teacher's
feedback
helps this
student know
what makes
her work
strong.

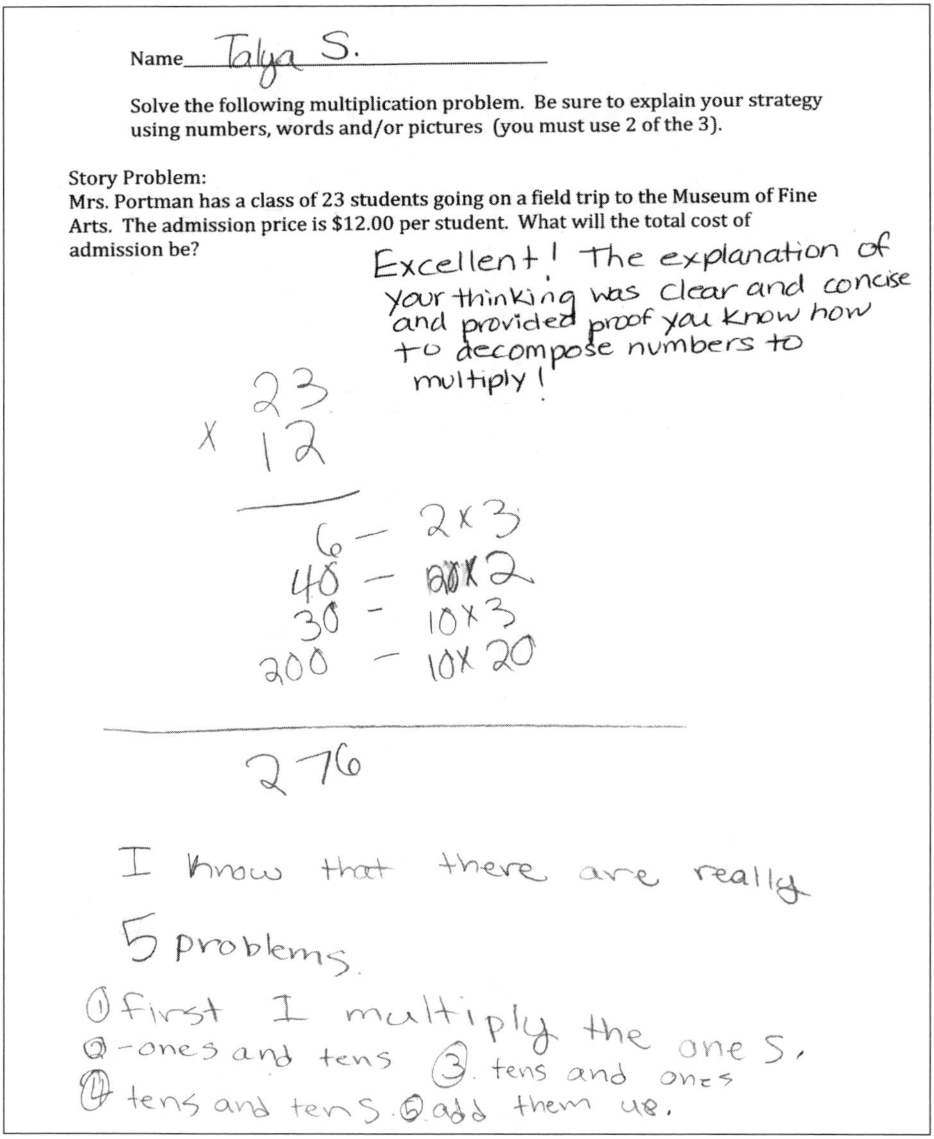

Name Talya S.

Solve the following multiplication problem. Be sure to explain your strategy using numbers, words and/or pictures (you must use 2 of the 3).

Story Problem:
Mrs. Portman has a class of 23 students going on a field trip to the Museum of Fine Arts. The admission price is $12.00 per student. What will the total cost of admission be?

Excellent! The explanation of your thinking was clear and concise and provided proof you know how to decompose numbers to multiply!

$$\begin{array}{r} 23 \\ \times\ 12 \\ \hline \end{array}$$

6 — 2 × 3
40 — 20 × 2
30 — 10 × 3
200 — 10 × 20

276

I know that there are really 5 problems.
① First I multiply the ones.
② -ones and tens ③. tens and ones
④ tens and tens. ⑤ add them up.

In Figure 3.8, the teacher provided a justified positive comment and recommended how the student could strengthen his answer: "Nice work! It was easy to follow your jumps on the number line. Next time you might want to write a number sentence combining all of your jumps."

Of course, the value of feedback is intensified in classrooms where the teacher has explicitly taught students how to read, interpret, and use the feedback. When students take the time to read and internalize the comments a teacher has taken the time to write, the payoff is big.

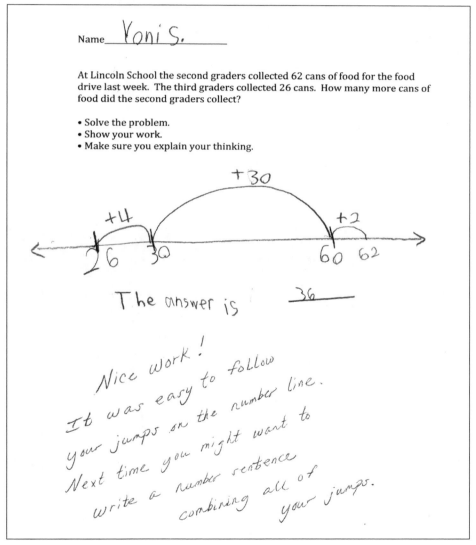

Figure 3.8: Yoni has positive feedback on his work as well as a constructive suggestion of what to do next.

6. USING WAIT TIME

◗ *What*

Most elementary teachers, myself included, employ wait time to some degree, yet we find it challenging to do so consistently for the appropriate amount of time. What is wait time, and what amount of wait time is optimal? It is the time between asking a question and calling on an individual student, a group of students, or the whole class for a response. The term is credited to science educator Mary Budd Rowe. Her research began in the 1960s and continued for decades. It showed that the amount of wait time in typical classrooms averaged less than one second. She identified two different intervals of wait time in her work: the first is the time between when the teacher asks a question and calls for a response and the second is the time between the student's response and the teacher's response to the student. Rowe further found that many positive results are to be seen when wait time increases to three to five seconds (1986), results that have been replicated and supported by others (Tobin 1987). (See Figure 3.9.)

A while back, a colleague videotaped me as I taught a lesson. Even though I was not initially looking at my use of wait time, it quickly became

Figure 3.9: As a result of the teacher providing ample wait time, these students have time to gather their thoughts and respond accordingly.

clear that I had some work to do in this area. Even on those occasions when I waited longer than one or two seconds after I asked a question, it was obvious that I was struggling against my inner need to fill the silence and not "waste" time. This experience opened my eyes, and I identified the need for more wait time as a priority in my practice. While I am better at holding back now, it is still something I have internal conversations about as I work to see the power of the silence.

So here's a challenge for you. Have a colleague observe you to see how much wait time you consistently use, and check out the results. You may find that one of my strategies will work for you. I use the old childhood count—one, one-hundred; two, one-hundred; three, one-hundred—and find that it works fairly well. In addition, I wait in silence, and then state, "I will wait until ten more hands are up," before continuing. These actions have helped me build more wait time into my practice and may do the same for you.

▶ Why

The purposes of using wait time are

- to lengthen responses from single words to complete statements,
- to increase student–student interaction,
- to allow more students to enter into the discussion,
- to decrease "I don't know" responses, and
- to increase students' confidence level (Rowe 1986).

▶ When

Anytime you ask a question, employ wait time and enjoy the silence, thinking of all the good that will come from it.

▶ *Magnification*

As every teacher knows, there is so much pressure (much of it internal) to move things along, to fit everything in, and to get the job done. It often feels as though eons have passed between when you asked a question and when students responded. As the time ticks in your head, you're thinking about how much you need to accomplish; you begin to worry about getting to the next part of the day while also worrying that you are losing momentum in the lesson and losing the attention of some of the students.

No wonder, then, that the words of Mrs. Matos, a fourth-grade teacher, resonate with so many:

I was made aware by my principal that I was averaging not even one second of wait time between when I asked a question in a whole-class lesson and then started calling on students for answers. I was dumb-founded and in disbelief, and I thought she must be mistaken—that I actually gave much more time than that. I had a friend and colleague come in to observe me for a math lesson and watch just for wait time. Even though I knew she was there for that reason, I still fell within the one- to one-and-a-half-second range! I was horrified! Since then, I have worked so hard to stop and wait. I have tried the counting thing, and it does help. I have also told my class that I have set a goal for myself in terms of wait time, and I think this has helped as well. I find that I am not rushing to fill the silences, and the kids know and feel this.

Keep in mind that the "silences" of wait time may not be so silent after all. They, indeed, can be quite noisy with the whir of student thinking.

7. SETTING AND SHARING LESSON GOALS/OBJECTIVES

◗ *What*

Setting and sharing the goals/objectives of a lesson are critical elements of mathematics instruction, as you most likely learned in Methods of Teaching 101. But why is this so? Take a minute and think about the lessons you have coming up this week; think of the goals you have set and could share with your students. Let's set this two-part component in context.

In *Understanding by Design*, Grant Wiggins and Jay McTighe (1998) brought this component to the foreground. The authors have extended their work in subsequent years and continue to do a phenomenal job helping teachers think about shaping both units of study and individual lessons. They began by offering a view of teachers as "designers" of both curriculum and assessment. They continue to urge teachers to work backward in this design process; instead of focusing initially on how you might plan a unit or a lesson using the textbook or familiar and favorite activities or lessons, start instead with thinking about what it is you want your students to know and be able to do by the end of the unit or lesson. Wiggins and McTighe formalize this "backward design process" in three stages: (1) identify desired results, (2) determine acceptable evidence, and (3) plan learning experiences and instruction (1998, 9). They then flesh out what it takes to work through each stage. Engaging in a backward design process will help you analyze your teaching, hone your thinking, and refine your practice.

▶ *Why*

The purposes of setting and sharing lesson goals/objectives are

- to help you to clarify your purpose and focus your planning,
- to give evidence of planning and purpose,
- to give students an anticipatory "heads up" as to what is expected,
- to give students ownership of their own learning,
- to give students an opportunity to reflect on what was done, and
- to connect lesson closure with lesson introduction.

▶ *When*

It is optimal to refer to the lesson goals or objectives at the start of the lesson by reading and pointing to them (as previously stated, these can be on a whiteboard, easel, sticky note, overhead projector, or document camera). Referring to them once again at the end of the lesson is a way to reflect on what was accomplished during the lesson.

▶ *Magnification*

This is a component that makes sense for both larger units of study as well as for individual lessons. Granted, you may be thinking that your school, district, and state have already identified what the goals are at an overall level, and the commercial program or textbook you may be using sets the goals at the beginning of each lesson for you. So why, then, this section? The key is that you begin with those expressed goals, tweak them in a way that fits the needs of your students, and allow yourself time to place these specific lesson goals in the context of the bigger picture. The next step is just as critical—sharing these goals for the unit or lesson with students. Your mission should not be a secret. Students deserve to know the intent of the lesson. I suggest sharing in both written and oral forms so the goals are publicized for all to see and hear. You be the judge of the language you use, depending on your students' grade level. Don't say, "Prove the commutative property of addition" to kindergartners; rather, you might write and say, "Show that 2 + 3 is the same as 3 + 2." Do not be reluctant, however, to use mathematical terms and vocabulary set in the context of the lesson, as this enhances the likelihood of students using such vocabulary with precision and accuracy.

By sharing your goals at the beginning of a lesson, you have included the students as agents in their own learning; they become more "mindful." A fourth-grade teacher put a relatively simple goal on the board at the start of a recent lesson for all to see—to "calculate without pencil/paper" (see Figure 3.10). She explicitly referred to it as the lesson began, at points throughout the lesson, and at the end of the lesson. By circling back to these goals at the end of the lesson, you signal to students that assessing for themselves on whether they met the goals as a class and as individuals is important. Of course, this is not the only way to determine whether goals have been met. As you know, just because a child says he "learned" something or "can do" something, self-reporting is only one component of assessment.

Figure 3.10: Fourth-grade teacher Susan Dyrek sets and shares the goals of the lesson.

This chapter revolves around the look of the lesson and focuses on what teachers might be seen doing in classrooms where rich mathematics is happening. There is quite a bit happening. I hope that when you envision such a classroom, you now see more because you are looking for more. I hope that you see teachers differentiating instruction and checking for understanding as the lesson proceeds and that you see them facilitating mathematical thinking by modeling it themselves and then fostering it in students. I hope that you also see them encouraging, motivating, and inspiring their students through countless moves and actions.

Let's now focus more closely on the look of students and examine what they might be doing during the lesson that strengthens their mathematical learning.

CHAPTER

4

THE LOOK OF THE LESSON: STUDENTS

Mathematics is not a spectator sport.

This statement has been around for a long time; it's the title of a book, it's quoted in countless articles, and it can be found on pencils, posters, mugs, and t-shirts. Basically, the message is that the best way to *learn* mathematics is to *do* mathematics. Yet what does "doing" mathematics look like? The *what, why,* and *when* of some of these actions will be discussed in this chapter, setting each into the context of a rich mathematical learning environment. Again, I caution that the following are but some of the actions we want to see students doing:

1. Actively engaging
2. Actively listening
3. Collaborating
4. Making connections

5. Persevering
6. Using what they know to find what they don't know
7. Taking risks

1. ACTIVELY ENGAGING

▶ *What*

Students need to be actively engaged, both mentally and physically (Figure 4.1). No doubt you know the look that crosses a student's face as he or she wrestles with an idea, seeking to make a connection. You can almost see the child's zone of proximal development spread on either side of him as he struggles to make sense of the new input on his way to new learning. This "zone" is part of Lev Vygotsky's learning theory and describes the difference between what a student can do independently in problem solving and what he or she can do with support and guidance. His theory supports students' active engagement with teachers as collaborators in the learning process (Vygotsky 1978). When a student is actively engaged, she experiences disequilibrium (Piaget 1959) that forces the creation of a new cognitive structure. You also know—but it never hurts to be reminded—that active physical engagement with manipulatives, with pictorial representations, with their own bodies, and with other students help children learn.

Figure 4.1: Actively engaged students in Brenda Malone's first-grade classroom

▶ *Why*

The purposes of the active mental and physical engagement of students are

- to create cognitive dissonance in order to create new learning and
- to provide students with multiple opportunities to engage with materials to explore and discover relationships from the concrete to the abstract.

▶ *When*

A lesson without the active mental and physical engagement of students is most likely a lesson without any real learning. Set the expectation right from the start that each student must come to school ready to be both hands-on and minds-on in their own learning.

▶ *Magnification*

After a brief whole-class lesson in Mr. Lopez's fourth-grade classroom, the students were charged with solving this problem:

> *A square table can seat 4 students. Two square tables placed together can seat 6 students. Using this arrangement, how many can be seated with 3, 10, 50, and 100 tables? Can you find a "rule" to help solve this problem for any number of tables? Show your work and explain your thinking.*

The students were set to work in pairs, with one partner solving the problem and writing their solution strategy in words and the other partner representing it with diagrams or tables. Before releasing them to begin their work, Mr. Lopez stated that one partner *had* to draw the diagram and the other *had* to write the explanation of their thinking and work. He reminded the students that they had done such a division of labor the prior week and asked them to model the same working partnerships. Mr. Lopez also stressed that both partners had to agree on what to draw and write.

Because each student had a responsibility as a partner and as an individual, both *had* to be involved. The students got to work as Mr. Lopez walked around to give on-the-spot coaching when needed. Most teams immediately sought a manipulative—among them square-inch tiles, base ten blocks, centimeter cubes, and geoboards. One team used square-inch tiles and base ten blocks to solve the problem by first acting it out. They designated the base ten flat (a 10 × 10) as the table and then used the square tiles as people around the table. They "built" the scenario for one table, then two, three, and even for ten tables. At that point, they decided to create a "rule":

Amelia: This is going to take way too long to do for 50 and 100.
Manuel: No kidding, and besides, we don't have enough flats anyway.
Amelia: So Mr. Lopez told us to look for a rule to help us.
Manuel: A pattern?
Amelia: Kind of. Let's look at the numbers. One table gives us 4 people.
Manuel: And 2 makes 6 and 3 makes 8, so they go up by 2.
Amelia: Yeah, but it would be a pain to write all the way up to 100 adding 2 each time. We have to look for something else.
Manuel: Let's make a table—not one to eat at—the other math kind.

And so they do, and as they continue to puzzle out the solution, they are huddled together on the floor, throwing ideas back and forth, with both students completely engaged mentally and physically. This kind of engagement does not come instantly, and we know some days are better than others. Nor does it come without the support of Mr. Lopez who knows the value of setting active engagement as an expectation, of "catching" students doing this and acknowledging it, of both modeling and reinforcing the idea that optimal learning takes place as a result of authentic engagement. The students knew they had to "buy in" to the idea that individual engagement was not optional. Mr. Lopez had been quite clear about that. No surprise that Mr. Lopez's meaningful and well-placed comments ("Wow! Look at the two of you go! You moved each other away from your initial plan to a more efficient one.") had an immediate positive impact, one I am sure that extended beyond that day.

2. ACTIVELY LISTENING

‣ *What*

Active listening is a set of behaviors that indicate "real listening" by one person in relation to another and is used not only in education but also in business and in medicine. As it is important that you are an active listener to your students, it is just as critical that students are active listeners. They should be engaged in the same actions you use to demonstrate listening by ingesting what is said, internalizing it, and then applying it. Whether the speaker is you or a classmate, students should maneuver their bodies to face the speaker. In addition, students should look at the speaker and establish periodic eye contact, as this helps students focus. Students should also have open, receptive, and nonthreatening posture.

▶ Why

The purposes of students actively listening are

- to give the speaker the message that what he or she has to say is important,
- to have students give that same message to other students,
- to provide students with the chance to communicate and clarify their thinking with the support of classmates, and
- to provide students with the chance to "see" how others think.

▶ When

You would like to think that students actively listen to you and to their classmates throughout the day. This is rarely the case, however, even for adults. You want them actively listening when you set the goals for a lesson, as you introduce new material, and when you give directions for task completion. You most definitely want to see them actively listening as their classmates share their thinking, their hypotheses, their solution paths, their observations, and their questions.

▶ *Magnification*

An activity I call "Twins" is adaptable to many different grade levels and to many different manipulatives (base ten blocks, centimeter cubes, geoboards, pattern blocks, for example). In this instance, every student in a second-grade classroom worked on this activity with a partner using pattern blocks. Students were directed to take turns and make some sort of a shape using no more than twelve pattern blocks, doing so behind a barrier such as a "table tent" to obstruct the partner's view. Each partner then had to describe to the other how he or she could construct the "twin" using only words and no hand gestures. They had done a similar activity before, and so the students knew they had to listen to the descriptions and directions given by their partners. (See Figure 4.2.)

Figure 4.2: To complete the "Twins" activity, these students in Jill Leonard's second-grade classroom must actively listen to one another.

Kaneiruh: There are 8 blocks in all. Get 3 yellow hexagons, 4 rhombuses, and 1 trapezoid.

Diego: What kind of rhombuses—fat or skinny?

Kaneiruh: The white ones. (She waits while Diego gets the blocks and then continues.) We're sorta making a person who has a hat on his head. You have to line up all of the hexagons so that one is kinda like the head, one is the top body, and the other is the bottom body.

Diego: Do they touch each other?

Kaneiruh: Yup. One whole side touches one whole side of the next one in the line.

Diego: Okay, got it, I think. What's next?

Next is completing the description with the two arms and two legs represented by the white rhombi. The tricky part was positioning them correctly against the trunk of the "body"; a few clarifying questions were asked and answered back and forth between partners. This is a prime example of students actively listening to one another, hanging on to each other's words. Diego had to listen actively to follow Kaneiruh's directions. Kaneiruh had to listen actively to respond to his clarifying questions.

To listen actively is a learned behavior. With the Twins activity, active listening is part of the lesson—the goal cannot be accomplished without students listening carefully to one another. Direct instruction can support general active listening, as illustrated by the kindergarten teacher who began the year with a class discussion on what makes a "good listener." While I understand the potential limitations of using the word *good*, it worked well in this class and may work well in yours. The class generated a list together; the teacher subsequently made a poster listing the actions, while some students drew corresponding pictures. The poster was placed on the wall in the meeting area. The students role-played which actions made a good and active listener and which did not. This took some time at the beginning of the year, but it was time well spent. Active student listening also can be fostered by asking the class after a student has spoken such questions as, "Who can tell us what Maria just said?" "Can you add one more thing to what was just said?" or "What do you agree with?"

3. COLLABORATING

▶ *What*

Collaborating describes actions that occur when students team up, work together, or join forces as they seek to solve problems and complete tasks. Dacey and Lynch (2007) offer a useful overview and description of what collaboration looks like in the elementary classroom. They provide techniques that you can easily use to foster collaborating:

- Students turn to their partners and tell their predictions.
- Student partners sit across from one another and share materials as they work to solve problems.
- Students develop a list of "partner behaviors" to be posted, which includes the following:
    Ask questions.
    Don't tell answers.
    Give hints.
    Respect each other.
    Listen attentively.
    Each takes responsibility (139).

When these actions are displayed in your classroom, you have students truly collaborating to get the job done.

◗ *Why*

The purposes of students collaborating are

- to improve the quality of students' interactions,
- to have students view themselves as both learners and teachers, and
- to have students experience that two (or more) minds can bring more power.

◗ *When*

Collaboration is usually easier to establish with students working in pairs. Initially, each student connects with only one other student (see Figure 4.3). Of course, there are times when collaboration can be seen in larger groups and even at the whole-class level.

◗ *Magnification*

As with every learning experience, it is not enough to *say* to your students that you will be looking for a certain behavior or action (although it would be great to have that kind of power). If you expect to observe students consistently working *with* one another to complete a task you have set, then specificity and modeling can be helpful.

Figure 4.3: To these fifth graders, collaboration is the key to completing the task successfully.

Ms. Wang: Gloriana and Max are going to share their predictions about whether the distance between our classroom and the cafeteria is greater than or less than 100 feet. Remember the EEK method we've used? Let's watch and listen as they turn and talk to each other—eye to eye, elbows resting, knee to knee.

Gloriana: I think it is less than 100 feet because that's 100 rulers and that's pretty long.

Max: I think it will be greater. Our room is at least 20 feet long, and I think there are more than five of our classrooms between here and the cafeteria.

Encourage collaboration by having a pair of students share one pencil, especially if each student is charged with recording their shared work.

4. MAKING CONNECTIONS

▶ *What*

Connections is one of the process standards in *Principles and Standards for School Mathematics* (National Council of Teachers of Mathematics 2000). NCTM believes that instructional programs should result in students being able to do the following:

- Recognize and use connections among mathematical ideas
- Understand how mathematical ideas interconnect and build on one another to produce a coherent whole
- Recognize and apply mathematics in contexts outside of mathematics (NCTM 2000, 64)

The underlying principles of this standard fit well with many of the mathematical practices identified in the *Common Core State Standards for Mathematics* (Common Core State Standards Initiative 2010). When students identify and then use connections between mathematical ideas, they are more likely to "make sense of problems and persevere in solving them" (Mathematical Practice 1). When students comprehend how mathematical ideas interconnect and build on one another, they must often "reason abstractly and quantitatively" (Mathematical Practice 2), analyzing the parts of a problem and how each part fits into the whole in order to understand and solve. This also allows them to "construct viable arguments and critique the reasoning of others" (Mathematical Practice 3) as they build on interconnected ideas and principles to understand other students' thinking.

▶ *Why*

The purposes of students making connections are

- to foster students' deeper conceptual understanding,
- to help students see how mathematical ideas are related, and
- to foster the idea that mathematics is important to all.

▶ *When*

Making connections is critical, not only during mathematics instruction but also throughout the day. By showcasing the connections that you make as you make them, celebrating the ones that students make, and remaining ever vigilant about how mathematical ideas and concepts impact you throughout the day, you are serving your students well. Put your students on alert and have them share when and where they are making such connections and the rewards will be bountiful.

▶ *Magnification*

When students "see" how $\frac{1}{2}$ of a candy bar is the same as $\frac{5}{10}$ of that bar and that it is also 50 percent of it, then you know that they are "getting" the idea that mathematics is not just a collection of discrete rules, laws, and procedures but instead consists of related ideas and concepts. You want them to connect that the patterns they see in counting from 0 to 100 lay the foundation for the patterns they see in counting from 100 to 200 and so on. The connection shows that they have grasped the iterative nature of the number system.

Making connections to the everyday world is another critical piece, as evidenced by a kindergartner who has made the connection between what a half means in math and what it means in his real world (Figure 4.4):

Ms. Doyle: What do you know about a half?
Charlie: Last night me and my brother, Will, wanted the last brownie. My mom said one of us gets to cut it. We both wanted to.
Ms. Doyle: How did the problem get solved?
Charlie: Well, Mom said that one of us cuts and the other one gets to pick first.
Ms. Doyle: Why do you think she did that?
Charlie: Because that way it would be fair.

Figure 4.4: Kindergartner Charlie makes the connection between the importance of equality and sharing a brownie with his brother.

Ms. Doyle: Tell me more.

Charlie: Well, I got to cut it, and I made sure I did it so the pieces were *really* even steven 'cause that's what half means.

Ms. Doyle could see that Charlie understands that dividing something in half is based on the principle of equality and that he could prove it with a real-world application.

5. PERSEVERING

▶ *What*

Sometimes it's hard to persevere when a task may seem too complex, too long, or too overwhelming. This, obviously, happens quite frequently with students. It is, therefore, all the more wonderful to watch a student stick to a task that is taking far longer than first anticipated (Figure 4.5); to see a student willingly return to a problem after getting an incorrect answer; and to

Figure 4.5: A third grader has dug in and is doing his best thinking on a challenging problem.

observe a student who used to say, "I don't get it!" when she couldn't solve a problem in the first ten seconds instead make two lists about the problem: "Things I know" and "Things I don't know and need to know."

▶ Why

The purposes of students persevering are

- to prove to students that they are more capable than they believe themselves to be as problem solvers,

- to foster independence, and
- to solidify the belief that persistence and perseverance pay.

▶ *When*

As a teacher, one of your many goals is to prepare your students to see that lifelong learning requires perseverance. Looking for the budding signs of perseverance in each student and acknowledging growth at every opportunity is a wonderful gift to give to your students.

▶ *Magnification*

No one can discount the importance of perseverance in learning and, yes, in life. For many students, solving math problems quickly defines a good mathematician. What can you do to underscore for your students that sticking with a mathematical task, pushing themselves, and finding a way around roadblocks to solve the problem will serve them well? What can you do to help your students internalize this core belief and to see that it is possible to push, push, push and come out on the other side? A few suggestions follow:

- Begin by outlawing the phrase "I don't get it!" No one is allowed to say it. Not ever! Instead, encourage students to state: "This is what I *do* get" (or know or understand or see) or "This is where I get stuck." Have them learn how to say this alone and then with a partner.
- Institute classroom routines to help with frustration:
  "Count to 10 and try again!" (Sometimes it is helpful to step away, take a breath, and go back to the problem.)
  "Read again and ask a friend." ("Real-life" mathematicians ask other mathematicians for help solving difficult problems. Students can do the same.)
  "Write what you know so you can go" (Recognizing that there are things that are known can be affirming enough to move on with one's thinking.)
- Recognize and praise students who stick to a task. (Adding something like the following can be motivating: "I saw that you really stuck with that problem even though it was hard. You didn't give up! It was good thinking on your part to take a break from the problem and then come back to it. When you came back, it seemed as if you were ready to try it again!")

6. USING WHAT THEY KNOW TO FIND WHAT THEY DON'T KNOW

◗ *What*

Using what you know to find out what you don't know is an efficient and elegant way to learn. Capitalizing on what's already in your knowledge bank can lead you to learn something new. This is what you want to see your students doing: taking advantage of information, discerning patterns, distilling various components, and then integrating the pieces to create new learning.

◗ *Why*

The purposes of students using what they know to find what they don't know are

- to help strengthen mathematical connections,
- to underscore the critical nature of looking for patterns, and
- to highlight the spiraling integration of mathematical ideas.

◗ *When*

I always began each year as a classroom teacher making this a class mantra:

*We must use what we know
To find out what we don't know!*

I posted this mantra in a visible spot and infused it into every lesson. Of course, you do not want to overuse the phrase so that it becomes meaningless. You do, however, want to heighten your awareness to look for evidence of it in student work and then to share it with the class.

◗ *Magnification*

It is exciting to see students pull from something they have previously learned and use it to build a bridge, providing for themselves a scaffold to discover something previously unknown.

Look at this third-grade student's solution to finding 4 × 15, a number combination with which he was unfamiliar (Figure 4.6). Judah did not know 4 × 15, but he did know the "doubles" and wrote "double 15 is 30" as

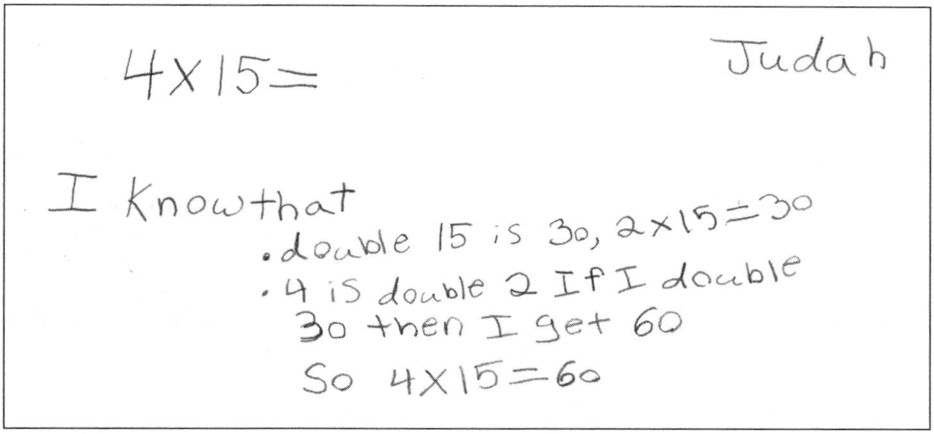
4X15=
Judah
I Knowthat
• double 15 is 30, 2x15=30
• 4 is double 2 If I double
30 then I get 60
So 4X15=60

Figure 4.6: Judah does not let what he doesn't know stop him from solving 4 × 15 right away; he capitalizes on what he does know to find the answer.

well as "2 × 15 = 30." He also knew that 4 is double 2, so "If I double 30, I will have the answer to 4 × 15; 4 × 15 = 60." I am sure you can envision Judah's face when his teacher commented, "It is so clear how you used what you already knew and applied that to find something you did not know at first. Do you feel proud of yourself?"—and of course, he did!

This evidence of a student using what he knows to find something he does not know is part of the joy that comes with teaching—watching a student come alive with the knowledge that he has the power to build bridges to further his own understanding.

7. TAKING RISKS

➧ *What*

Imagine how happy you would be if you saw every child in your class poised and ready to take a risk with his or her own learning. What would that look like? (See Figure 4.7.) You would see a student taking a chance, sharing with the class how he solved a problem even though he was unsure whether he had arrived at the correct solution. You would observe a student saying, "Oh, maybe I could try it this way . . . since that other way did not work!" and doing so with pride that she came up with another strategy. You would see a student saying, "I'll try," when asked to show a classmate why he knows his strategy works.

Figure 4.7: This is a risk well worth taking for these two kindergartners as they explain their solution for the "problem of the day" to their classmates. Smiles abound!

◗ Why

The purposes of students taking risks are

- to have students see that their trust in you and their classmates is well founded,
- to increase students' self-confidence, and
- to underscore that risks often come with learning and that learning always comes with risks.

◗ When

Whenever and wherever they can . . .

◗ Magnification

During the discussion and closure of a third-grade lesson, Mrs. Bazath had noticed that Tashika started to put her hand up a couple of times and then pulled it back and lowered her head. The class had been working on angles and how to apply the measures of the "friendly" angles to the everyday world; for example, the measure of a doorway to the floor is 90 degrees. They had also seen how angles are shown on the coordinate plane. The third time Tashika put up her hand and then almost immediately started to put it down, Mrs. Bazath called on Tashika.

Mrs. Bazath: Tashika, I can see that you have something to add.

Tashika: I'm not sure if it makes sense.

Mrs. Bazath: Do you want to give it a try? Sometimes it makes more sense when we hear something out loud.

Tashika: I can try, but I'm still not sure.

Mrs. Bazath: Go for it.

Tashika: Okay. I get that a straight line is 180 degrees cuz it's like two 90s back to back. What I don't get—I'm just wondering—is a straight line still 180 degrees if it's diagonal?

Mrs. Bazath: What a great question, Tashika! I think it makes a lot of sense to ask this question. I also think that it took some courage on your part to ask it.

Mrs. Bazath continued to tease out Tashika's question with the class. Tashika rocked with excitement as the discussion continued. Tashika was filled with the knowledge that she had moved past her reluctance, put aside her fear that she was asking a "stupid" question, and took a chance. So how many Tashikas have you had? How many students do you have right now who are hesitant about taking a risk for fear of looking silly (or worse) in front of you or their peers? How many will raise a hand only if they are 100 percent confident that their answer is right? How many believe that unless their explanation is perfect, it does not really count? This is where your recognition of students taking risks and your support of them when doing so are of paramount importance.

Looking back on this chapter while envisioning a mathematically rich classroom, I hope that you see students who embody the idea that math is not a spectator sport. I hope that you see students who are productively busy in this classroom, engaging both mentally and physically as they actively listen to one another, collaborate and persevere, take risks and make connections, and use what they know to find what they don't know.

Let's now turn up the sound in this classroom and listen more closely to what students and teachers are saying—to the class, to a partner, to themselves.

CHAPTER

THE SOUND OF THE LESSON

What is honored in a country will be cultivated there.

—Plato

My earliest memory of a math class is from third grade. My teacher had us switch our homework with a neighbor and then called ten students to the board to complete the first set of homework problems on multiplying two 2-digit numbers. I was chosen, but I was so nervous (even though I knew I had the right answer since my father had checked my homework). We each completed our problem at the board, the teacher put either a check or an X next to it, and everyone did the same on the papers we were correcting. If a problem was wrong, the teacher made the correction on the board. She then gave us the answers for the next 15 problems, we marked our classmates' papers accordingly, put a score at the top of the paper, and she recorded each score. The teacher then told us she was going to show us how to multiply with three-digit numbers. She did a few examples on the board, asked if we had any questions (there were none), set us to do ten similar problems as "seatwork," and assigned us twenty-five problems for homework. Overall, it was a quiet class, not much to hear.

Fast-forward to my first teaching job. I had twenty-eight second graders, and I had been given a math workbook to complete. During my first year, I followed the teacher's guide and pretty much practiced the show/tell/do approach. I would show a problem, tell my students what to do to get the answer, and they did it. I figured out quickly that this was not going to work for all of my students, and I sought ways to help my students learn the concepts as well as the procedures. A quiet math class was not going to do the trick if I wanted my students to be actively involved in their own learning. Thus began my journey toward creating a classroom that buzzed with engaged talk and conversation.

Fast-forward to the present. My journey continues as I work to refine and expand on the elements I want to hear in a mathematics lesson. I want noise and plenty of it—productive, purposeful, and meaningful noise—from everyone, students and teachers alike. In this chapter, I will identify and amplify eight of these components, listening to what *teachers* might be saying, what *students* might be saying, and what *both teachers and students* might be saying.

The Sound of Teachers
1. Teachers supporting discourse
2. Teachers providing lesson summation/reflection/closure
3. Teachers engaging all students

The Sound of Students
4. Students justifying reasoning
5. Students analyzing the thinking of others

The Sound of Students and Teachers
6. Both students and teachers actively listening
7. Both students and teachers encouraging and modeling risk taking
8. Both students and teachers using mathematical vocabulary

THE SOUND OF TEACHERS

1. TEACHERS SUPPORTING DISCOURSE

♦ What

Supporting—initiating and sustaining—classroom discourse is something teachers want to do well. Supporting discourse means learning how to use both student and teacher language to deepen mathematical understanding and knowledge. Communication, as the expression of ideas, "is a way for students to articulate, clarify, organize, and consolidate their thinking" (National Council of Teachers of Mathematics [NCTM] 2000, 128). In the Common Core State Standards, several of the standards for mathematical practices draw from the proficiencies outlined in NCTM's communication standard and compose a good part of what should be heard in a classroom:

> *Mathematical Practice 1: Make sense of problems and persevere in solving them* (Common Core State Standards Initiative [CCSSI] 2010). If students are to succeed in doing this, they must first be able to communicate to themselves what a problem means and understand what they are being asked to do.
>
> *Mathematical Practice 3: Construct viable arguments and critique the reasoning of others* (CCSSI 2010). When students communicate clearly and articulate their ideas to others, their thinking becomes visible and their understanding deepens. Further, when students follow the thinking of others and communicate why they agree or disagree, their understanding often solidifies and strengthens.
>
> *Mathematical Practice 6: Attend to precision* (CCSSI 2010). This practice goes beyond attaining accurate answers to ensure that mathematically proficient students communicate with precision—that their language is clear, their reasoning can be followed, their words and symbols are unambiguous.

♦ Why

The purposes of teachers supporting discourse are

- to help students analyze problems and become more proficient problem solvers,
- to foster the idea that the explanation of one's thinking is critical to understanding,

RECOMMENDED RESOURCES

Classroom Discussions: Using Math Talk to Help Students Learn (Chapin, O'Connor, and Anderson 2009)
The authors provide invaluable support to promote skilled discourse in the elementary classroom. They outline five "productive talk moves" (revoicing, repeating, reasoning, adding one, and waiting) and offer detailed suggestions for implementation as you work to improve mathematical discussions in your classroom.

Math Exchanges: Guiding Young Mathematicians in Small-Group Meetings (Omohundro Wedekind 2011)
The author focuses on the mathematical learning that happens in small-group settings. In it, Omohundro Wedekind provides a big-picture context for understanding the critical nature of mathematical discourse—these "math exchanges," as she calls them, that yield rich results. In addition, she details how to plan for, implement, and reflect about these exchanges, while keeping the focus on "teaching the mathematician, not the math" (2011, 38).

- to promote clarity and precision in communicating student thinking and reasoning, and
- to inform instruction by gathering more information about students' understandings and misunderstandings or misconceptions.

◆ *When*

There are three settings when teachers can be heard supporting discourse: whole class, small group (Figure 5.1), and one on one.

Figure 5.1: Fifth-grade teacher Boris Samarov engages students in a discussion about the connection between area and perimeter.

◆ *Amplification*

Teachers can examine and change their own language to initiate, support, deepen, and extend the mathematical discourse in their classrooms. I have set this examination and process within a framework of four categories: Rephrase, Rewind, Review, and Recharge.

Rephrase

What	Why	Amplification
Teacher restates what a student has shared and verifies with student that the rephrase is accurate.	1. Validates for student that he has been heard by the teacher 2. Gives the student a chance to reflect and respond in order to clarify 3. Allows for possible clarification for other students through "reprocessing" by the teacher	1. I think I heard you say . . . Is that what you said? 2. You saw that . . . Did I understand that correctly? 3. So you believe that . . . Is that your thinking? 4. You solved it by . . . Did I follow your strategy right?

Rewind

What	Why	Amplification
Teacher asks other students to repeat what a classmate has said.	1. Validates for student that he has been heard by classmates 2. Allows for possible clarification for other students through "reprocessing" by classmates 3. Underscores the importance of listening	1. Who can give a rewind of what Marco just said? (*Rewind* has previously been defined, modeled, and used in the classroom.) 2. Take turns retelling to your partner what Alana just explained. 3. Who made a "recording" of Peter's thinking and can replay it? 4. Can someone restate Carla's explanation?

Review

What	Why	Amplification
Teacher asks other students to review and evaluate a student explanation to determine agreement or disagreement.	1. Underscores the importance of listening 2. Fosters analysis of others' reasoning to determine agreement or disagreement	1. Who can give a review of Jorge's thinking by telling if you agree or disagree and why? 2. What about Eduardo's idea makes sense to you? 3. Is there something about Sara's reasoning that you disagree with? Why? 4. Tell your partner what you think is the strongest part of Philippe's explanation.

Recharge

What	Why	Amplification
Teacher asks other students to "recharge" a student's explanation by adding to it.	1. Validates for student that his thinking is important and "buildable" 2. Underscores the importance of listening 3. Fosters analysis of others' reasoning to determine what might make it stronger 4. Invites wider participation in collaborative setting	1. Who can add to this? 2. Who would like to build on this idea? 3. Where can we go from here? 4. What other thoughts do you have?

2. TEACHERS PROVIDING LESSON SUMMATION/REFLECTION/CLOSURE

◆ *What*

Lesson summation usually takes place with either teachers or students summarizing and reflecting on the main points of a lesson (Figure 5.2). One way

Figure 5.2: Mrs. Dyrek closes the lesson by having students give examples of goals that were met.

to do this is to circle back to the lesson goals and objectives shared at the beginning of the lesson and address each one.

▶ Why

The purposes of providing lesson summation/reflection/closure are

- to determine whether lesson goals have been met;
- to highlight key information, skills, and ideas addressed in the lesson;
- to solidify understanding; and
- to transition to what comes next.

▶ When

Lesson summation/reflection/closure most often happens at the end of a lesson. It can be as short as two to three minutes, with five minutes as a good average. There are also times, however, when lesson summation fits well at the beginning of the next day's lesson, as a springboard for an upcoming connected lesson.

◗ *Amplification*

A third-grade teacher, Ms. Anderson, was closing a lesson with her class on using parentheses. It was right before the December holiday break, and students were eager for the start of vacation. Ms. Anderson had held their attention and included the students in every aspect of the lesson. She was tempted (she later admitted) to bring the lesson quickly to a close and move on to the next part of the day but resisted the urge and used five minutes to have students participate in the lesson closure.

Ms. Anderson (pointing to the goal written on the corner of the whiteboard): Let's look back at the goal we started with at the beginning of the lesson:

1. *To see how parentheses can change the value of a number sentence*

Ms. Anderson: Who would like to read this and tell the class if and how we met that goal? (She waits until almost all of the hands are up and calls on Giorgio.)

Giorgio: I have a hard time saying the word, but I know what they look like and I know what they do. (He starts to read the goal and struggles with "parentheses"; Ms. Anderson helps him with the rest of the word.) Yeah. *Par—en—the—ses*. It's easier if I stretch it out. Anyway, when they are there, they can make a number sentence mean something different than when they're not there.

Ms. Anderson: I see. Give a thumbs up if you see this as well. (She waits.) Who can pick up where Giorgio left off and add to this? (She takes note that many hands go up. She calls on Vanessa.)

Vanessa (begins by reading the goal aloud): We reached this goal—Billy and me—when we did our partner work.

Ms. Anderson: Can you give some evidence that changing the parentheses can change the value of a number sentence?

Vanessa: Yup. Can I come to the board? (She does.) Say, I have 4, 3, and 1, and I put a minus sign between the 4 and the 3 and a plus between the 3 and 1. I can get two different answers if I put the parentheses around the first two numbers or the last two. (She writes on the board.):

$$4 - 3 + 1 \text{ can be } (4 - 3) + 1 = 2 \text{ or}$$
$$4 - (3 + 1) = 0$$

So we know that the answer can change if the parentheses change.

Ms. Anderson: Vanessa described how she and Billy reached the lesson goal. Give a thumbs up if you and your partner had a similar experience. (She waits to see if all thumbs go up. They do.) Okay, so it seems as if we agree that we met the main goal of the lesson. Tomorrow we are going to do more work with parentheses as we write number models that match number stories.

3. TEACHERS ENGAGING ALL STUDENTS

◗ *What*

We all want to hear every student at some point sharing an idea, stating an opinion, putting forth a hypothesis, or describing a strategy. How does that happen? The responsibility for this type of engagement falls to the teacher. Remember my initial show/tell/do approach in which I, as the teacher, would show the students what to do, tell them how to do it, and then have them "do" as I had done? As I said, I figured out fairly quickly that this approach did not and does not work for all. I was treating my students as "listening objects," a term Paolo Freire (2000, 71) uses to describe students in this type of instructional setting, and I knew I wanted more for my students.

When I speak about "hearing" teachers engage all students, I am talking about how teachers use words to ensure their students are more than "listening objects." Further, by "students," I mean every student, not only the four or five who raise their hands every time a question is asked, and not only the "smart math kids." The goal is that all students are physically, cognitively, and affectively engaged (Figure 5.3).

RECOMMENDED RESOURCES

Total Participation Techniques: Making Every Student an Active Learner (Himmele and Himmele 2011)
The authors detail thirty-seven "classroom-ready TPTs [total participation techniques]," each of which can help improve teaching and learning by putting the focus on students being active in their learning.

Creating the Opportunity to Learn (Boykin and Noguera 2011)
While the focus is on closing the achievement gap between ethnic groups, the authors provide compelling research about factors that affect the achievement of all students. Their chapter on engagement illuminates this variable and places active student engagement as critical to student learning, while identifying avoidance strategies students sometimes employ.

Figure 5.3: Barbara Connearney ensures that her second-grade students stay connected to the lesson.

▶ Why

The purposes of engaging all students are

- to emphasize that "math is not a spectator sport,"
- to give a clear message that the ideas of all are valued,
- to foster a willingness to take risks,
- to create a classroom community of learners, and
- to build confidence as learners.

▶ When

Every lesson is filled with multiple opportunities to engage students. It is a matter of pulling students into the lesson at every possible point, moving them from the periphery to the core of their own learning.

▶ Amplification

There are many ways to pull students from passive recipients of information to active engagement on many levels: from my teacher show/teacher tell/

student do approach to a student show/student tell/student do scenario. Teachers can be heard saying the following:

What	Why	Amplification
Partner think & share	Allows time for each student to reflect individually first and then share with a partner and possibly with the class	When you are ready, turn to your partner and share your thinking.
Thumbs up when good to go	Gives message that students have some time to think, followed by a low-risk signal	Give a thumbs up when you are ready to share (or start to work, etc.)—good to go.
Hands up	Gives a chance for students to think first and give some thought to whether they agree or disagree	Hold up one hand if you agree, two hands if you disagree. Be ready with the "why."
Write/draw (on individual whiteboards or paper)	Provides a chance for students to write or draw their thinking, supporting various learning styles as well as time for thinking	Give it some time and then record your thinking with words, numbers, or pictures.
Hearing from the unheard	Sends a signal that notice is being taken of who has shared and who has not, underscoring that all voices are important	Let's hear from a voice that hasn't been heard yet.
Heads-up sharing	Can give a reluctant oral participant confidence in advance of sharing	I saw that Inez has a creative solution, and I have asked her to share it.
True/false two-step	Allows for bodily movement as students (whole class or group) stand, think, and move	Take two steps forward if you think _____ is true or two steps backward if you think it is false.

THE SOUND OF STUDENTS

4. STUDENTS JUSTIFYING REASONING

▶ *What*

When students explain how they have arrived at an answer, they often recite the steps they took and leave it at that. Justifying their reasoning, however, goes beyond describing what they have done. To justify reasoning, we must prove it, validate it, rationalize it, defend it, and substantiate it. NCTM holds reasoning and proof as "fundamental aspects of mathematics" (NCTM 2000, 56) and urges that teachers fold them into every lesson. The critical nature of reasoning is further accentuated by CCSSI's Mathematical Practice 2, "Reason Abstractly and Quantitatively" (2010). It spills over to Mathematical Practice 3 as well in the construction of "viable arguments," asking that educators place a premium on students explaining their reasoning beyond a retelling of the process they followed to solve a problem.

There are multiple facets of students justifying their reasoning. Rathouz (2011) presents three helpful strategies that effectively support student reasoning and justification of their reasoning: "invent a way," "imagine an alternative," and "compare and contrast." Rathouz provides an overview of how to incorporate these strategies into everyday practice. She explains that when students invent a way to solve a problem, they are often placed in the position of explaining to their peers why their answer makes sense and why it works, forcing them to deconstruct and defend their own thinking (see Figure 5.4 for one student's example). When they are asked to imagine an alternative, they are presented with an answer that is different from one already given and are asked to think about why and how someone could think it might be the correct answer; this also forces a deconstruction of reasoning as well as an analysis of possible errors. The compare and contrast strategy puts into place what we know to be higher-order thinking as students think about why something may work in one case but not in another, supporting conjectures based on reasoning.

▶ *Why*

The purposes of students justifying their reasoning are

- to move beyond "answer only" to higher-order thinking,
- to foster student articulation of thought processes,

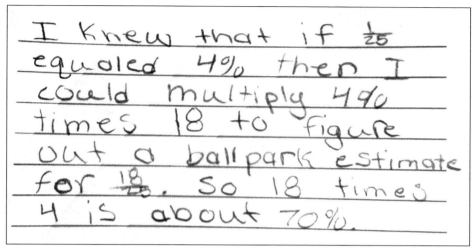

I knew that if $\frac{1}{25}$ equaled 4% then I could multiply 4% times 18 to figure out a ballpark estimate for $\frac{18}{25}$. So 18 times 4 is about 70%.

Figure 5.4: R.J. first gave an oral accounting of how he determined the approximate value of $\frac{18}{25}$ as a percent and then provided a written justification of his reasoning.

- to provide opportunities for shared learning and learning from peers, and
- to nurture the joy of looking for the "why" of mathematical ideas.

▶ When

Whether in a classroom as a teacher, a principal, or a student, one should hear the beautiful noise of students sharing their reasoning and proving why and how it makes sense in all sorts of settings—to the whole class, to a small group of peers, to a partner, to the teacher, or to a visitor.

▶ Amplification

Growing up in a family of eleven (I had seven younger siblings when I was ten!), there was quite a bit of noise (what an understatement). My mother had a strong background in literacy, and my father was an engineer. They both believed we should share our thoughts and ideas, and so we did—often quite loudly! We had a family "rule" that when you were asked why you did something or thought something, you were not allowed to say, "I don't know." Although it was frustrating at times, we became adept at giving reasons for our thoughts and actions. I took that ability with me into my first classroom and have worked to expand on it in my years as an educator.

Phrases that illustrate students justifying their reasoning (often in response to a teacher prompt) are presented here:

I know this works because . . .
This is an example of . . .
This is a "counterexample" that proves . . .
I can show you that it works . . .
Let me draw a picture to show that . . .
When I did this, _____ happened, so I know that . . .
I began by thinking _____ but saw that _____ so now I know that . . .
I saw that _____ worked here but not here, so I knew that . . .

5. STUDENTS ANALYZING THE THINKING OF OTHERS

▶ *What*

Analyzing others' thinking is a natural follow-up of students justifying their own reasoning. When a student listens to a peer explain the why and how of something he did and is then able to process and deconstruct her fellow classmate's explanation, then she is applying higher-level thinking, not just recalling information. Mathematical Practice 3 of the Common Core, "Construct Viable Arguments and Critique the Reasoning of Others," speaks to the importance of mathematically proficient students being able to do this. At first it may be challenging for younger elementary students to evaluate the thinking of others; however, they are capable of higher-order thinking, and the seeds for that kind of practice can be planted in the primary grades and fertilized along the way. If you have ever taught at a primary grade, see whether this sounds familiar: A student has just finished explaining his answer, and you ask, "Who solved it a different way than Daniel did?" Hands fly up and you choose someone who proceeds to describe the identical solution strategy as Daniel's! So I rephrase the question: "Who can tell me one thing they did the same as Daniel and one thing that was different?" It may not always work, but it does help students think about similarities and differences.

▶ *Why*

The purposes of students analyzing the thinking of others are

- to promote students listening to one another,

- to strengthen their own understanding of a concept/procedure, and
- to explore and probe both flawed and plausible arguments.

▶ *When*

This is again something you want to hear happening in multiple settings with students. It is especially powerful as a motivator when students engage in analyzing and critiquing the reasoning of others in the whole-class setting, as it serves as a potential model for other students. It is also beneficial for this to happen when students are working with one another in small groups or as partners.

▶ *Amplification*

Ms. Tanara had presented her second-grade class with several story problems, and each small group was assigned a specific problem. The teacher was taking advantage of the school's shared goal of helping students listen to one another, so that goal had been incorporated into her math lessons. Ms. Tanara called one of the groups together so that the four boys and two girls could discuss how each solved a story problem that involved adding a series of numbers. Ms. Tanara had set up the sharing session by telling the students that the first student would describe how and why he had solved the problem a certain way and that the next student had to mention one similarity and one difference in his solution strategy.

Yoni: I knew I had to add all eight numbers, so I wrote them down on my whiteboard (Figure 5.5):

    4 7 5 9 2 11 3 10

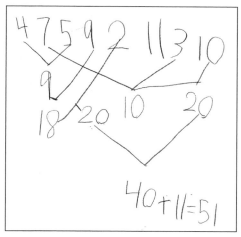

Figure 5.5: Yoni's solution strategy

I then put 7 and 3 together to make 10.
Then I added the other 10 to make 20.
That left 4, 5, 9, 2, and 11.
4 and 5 make 9. 9 and 9 are doubles and make 18. 18 and 2 more make 20. 20 and my other 20 are doubles and make 40. Then add 11 to 40 and I got 51.

Ms. Tanara: Yoni, thank you for the explanation of your thinking. If you understand how Yoni solved this, give a thumbs up. (She waits—all five give a thumbs up.) Who solved it doing at least one thing the same as Yoni and one thing different? (She waits and calls on Nevo who had raised his hand.)

Nevo: I looked for tens just like Yoni did and saw that 7 and 3 make 10 like he did (Figure 5.6).

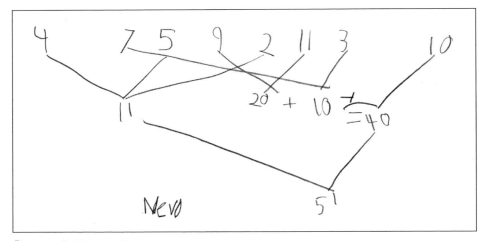

Figure 5.6: Nevo's solution strategy

Then I looked for more tens. I took one away from the 11 and gave it to the 9 and that gave me 2 more tens so now I have 30. Add the 10 on the end and I have 40. All I had left was 4 and 5 and 2 and they make 11 and 11 and 40 make 51.

Ms. Tanara: I see. You explained your reasoning clearly. Who can share what Yoni and Nevo did that was the same and what was different? (Hands go up. Rachel is called on to share.)

Rachel: So Yoni and Nevo, they both looked for ways to 10. I did that, too. It's easy for me to work with tens. But then they both did different stuff. I got the way that Yoni did it, but I'm not sure about how Nevo did.

Ms. Tanara: Can someone explain why Nevo "took one away from the 11 and gave it to the 9" and then tell if you think it is a good strategy?

Another student was able to explain the thinking behind Nevo's move as a "seesaw—if there are 9 kids on one side and 11 on the other, you make it even by moving one from the 11 side to the other side and that makes it even and it gives you double tens!"

Ms. Tanara accomplished a few things in this group exchange. She underscored the idea that listening to the thinking of others is valued in this classroom. She also presented the responsibility for listening to a student explain his thinking as a shared responsibility—both she and the other students were given a stake in this. The students knew that they had to listen to Nevo and Yoni so that they could determine how their own strategies were similar and dissimilar. This, as you know, is thinking at a higher level than simply recalling or retelling information. In addition, Ms. Tanara further encouraged students to be active in their own learning.

THE SOUND OF STUDENTS AND TEACHERS

6. BOTH STUDENTS AND TEACHERS ACTIVELY LISTENING

▶ *What*

While the Actively Listening section of Chapter 4 describes what we should see students *doing*, this section accentuates the *sound* of students and teachers actively listening—students to students, students to teacher, teacher to students (see Figure 5.7).

Figure 5.7: The teacher's and students' body language tells of their active listening to one another.

◗ *Why*

The purposes of students and teachers actively listening are

- to cultivate a classroom culture in which others' ideas are seen as valuable,
- to learn from one another and deepen individual understanding,
- to underscore that all students have something to offer, and
- to learn what students know and understand.

◗ *When*

Active listening takes place at all points throughout the lesson. A classroom where students listen to teachers set the stage for learning; where students listen to classmates in whole-class discussions whether at the beginning, middle, or end of a lesson; where students listen to their partners during paired work; and where teachers listen to students at all times is a place where learning is optimized.

◗ *Amplification*

Words and phrases that signal active listening is happening include the following:

Students
"I heard Isaiah say that . . ."
"I think that Ivantika solved it by . . ."
"I never thought about solving it the way Fernando did."

Teachers
"I heard you say that . . ."
"You made a strong point when you said . . ."
"If I used Katerina's strategy, it would go like this . . ."

7. BOTH STUDENTS AND TEACHERS ENCOURAGING AND MODELING RISK TAKING

◗ *What*

Taking risks is discussed in Chapter 4 as something students should be seen doing; it is included here to highlight the sound of both teachers and stu-

Figure 5.8: Supported by his teacher and classmates, a kindergartner expresses joy in taking a risk that everyone can see and hear.

dents (Figure 5.8) taking risks and encouraging risk taking in others. This happens when teachers and students move beyond their comfort zones and express their emotions aloud as they pursue understanding and learning.

◗ Why

The purposes of students and teachers taking risks and encouraging risk taking are

- to open up the learning field to all,
- to recognize that learning involves putting oneself "out there,"
- to applaud the efforts of others, and
- to strengthen the classroom as a community of learners.

◗ When

During a lesson, there are multiple opportunities to hear both teachers and students taking risks and encouraging others to do the same—whether in the whole-class setting, in small-group work, in pairs with other students or with the teacher.

◗ *Amplification*

These are some of the words and phrases I have both heard and said in a productive, noisy classroom that illustrate students and teachers taking risks, modeling taking risks, and encouraging others in taking risks:

Students
"I'm not sure but I think that . . ."
"This worked for the first problem, so I'm going to give it a try for this one."
"This isn't easy for me, but I'm going to do my best."
"I don't think anyone will agree with me, but I solved it by . . ."
"I think Saul gave a great answer when you called on him. He really had to think first though."

Teachers
"This is something I had to work on for a long time before I felt comfortable doing it with you."
"Even though Mia was nervous about adding to the discussion, she made us all think. Nice job!"
"Give yourself a moment and then take a chance!"
"You know this. Go ahead and give it a try!"
"Can you share part of your idea, even if you're not sure of your answer?"

8. BOTH STUDENTS AND TEACHERS USING MATHEMATICAL VOCABULARY

◗ *What*

In *Building Academic Vocabulary*, Marzano and Pickering (2005) maintain, and I and many others agree, that using and developing vocabulary are essential elements of academic achievement. "People's knowledge of any topic is encapsulated in the terms they know that are relevant to the topic" (Marzano and Pickering, 2005, 2). A body of research suggests that vocabulary is a key to closing the achievement gap. In any case, the correct use of mathematical vocabulary is integral to understanding mathematics. It is a prime component of Mathematical Practice 6, "Attend to Precision," as part of what mathematically proficient students do when they communicate their thinking and reasoning (CCSSI 2010). They use clear definitions, unambiguous language, and appropriate symbols that match their thinking—all of which are part of using mathematical vocabulary. Vocabulary used in context consistently, accurately, and appropriately by both students and teachers can build bridges to understanding and should be filling the airwaves in elementary classrooms.

▶ Why

The purposes of students and teachers using mathematical vocabulary are

- to promote clarity of communication,
- to level the playing field for students,
- to foster conceptual understanding, and
- to embed understanding in context.

▶ When

Every lesson that brims with mathematical vocabulary is an opportunity for understanding to flourish (see Figure 5.9).

Figure 5.9: Demonstrating and discussing types of angles

▶ *Amplification*

I like to think that mathematical vocabulary can act as a pump for math power. Instead of erecting barriers to understanding, vocabulary can help construct connectors to conceptual knowledge. According to the NCTM, students must have opportunities to use mathematical vocabulary and language in meaningful ways: "Language is as important to learning mathematics as it is to learning to read" (NCTM 2000, 128). Further, math vocabulary should not be taught out of context as a separate entity but rather be modeled and used every day. Of course, sometimes we're not as pure in our language choices as we should be. As Barnett-Clarke and Ramirez state beautifully, "As teachers, we must learn to carefully choose the language pathways that support mathematical understanding, and simultaneously, we must be alert for language pitfalls that contribute to misunderstandings of mathematical language" (2004, 56).

To that end, I am providing a few of what I call "muddy words and phrases" (see table on page 97). When teachers and students use these, they erect barriers to understanding at best or create misunderstandings at worst. I am sure you can add to the list, but I offer it as a starting point of words and phrases that we do not want to be part of our productively noisy classrooms.

It is time to reflect on some of the components that we hear in classrooms and that have been amplified in this chapter. Can you hear skilled discourse that includes all students? Are lessons coming full circle with closure that connects to the goals shared at the start of the lessons? Is every student purposely and deliberately invited into the action and engaged actively? Is students' thinking appreciated and their justified reasoning anticipated? Is the expectation that students must analyze and critique the thinking of others audible? Are both students and teachers actively listening to one another? Are the airwaves filled with rich mathematical vocabulary that enhances communication and understanding? Is everyone encouraged to take risks with their learning and to support others to do the same? Borrowing from Plato, is what you are hearing truly indicative of what you value and want to cultivate in classrooms?

Up to this point, we have focused on components of mathematics instruction that can be seen. Chapter 6 deals with components that are far less tangible yet still hold a central role in mathematics teaching and learning—the "feel" of it all.

Muddy Word/Phrase	Why It Is Muddy	Rephrase & Amplification
Borrow (when subtracting)	Implies a giving back—the ten is not "given back"	Rename/regroup Adding this to the other tens
You can't subtract 6 from 4.	Yes you can!	You have 4 dollars in your pocket and you owe your mother 6; if you pay her the 4, where are you then? (2 dollars in debt = −2)
Carry (when adding)	Is the student really "carrying" that ten?	Regroup
Reduce	Reduce means to make smaller. Is $\frac{1}{2}$ smaller than $\frac{5}{10}$?	Simplify Write in lowest terms
Less/fewer	Often used interchangeably but should not be; *fewer* refers to separate, discrete, distinct items; *less* refers to continuous variables	Paulo has ten fewer blocks than Diego has. Paulo's glass is less than half full.
Digit vs. number vs. numeral	Often used interchangeably, yet are different:	
	Digit—one of the 10 symbols in our number system	0, 1, 2, 3, 4, 5, 6, 7, 8, 9 are the ten digits in our number system.
	Number—a mathematical object used to count, measure, or identify	I have 4 brothers. The difference between 5 and 3 is 2. My telephone number is 555-1234.
	Numeral—a symbol used to represent a number	2 is the numeral in our number system used to represent the number 2 (just as II is the Roman numeral for 2).
Just add 0 when multiplying by 10	When you add 0 to a number, you end up with the same number, not ten times that number.	When you multiply a number by 10, you increase the value 10 times; you change the value by one place.

CHAPTER

THE FEEL OF IT ALL

*The more we help children have their wonderful ideas and feel good
about themselves for having them, the more likely it is they will
someday happen upon ideas that no one else has happened upon before.*

—Eleanor Duckworth

Regardless of whether you are a teacher or an administrator, you know when you walk into a classroom whether it is a place where children can thrive, have good ideas, and feel good about themselves for having those good ideas. Within a short time, you can "feel" whether a classroom environment supports all students as they grow in their learning and whether the teacher engages children both cognitively and affectively.

Anyone who has ever taught math knows that affective considerations—feelings and attitudes—greatly influence student performance. What can teachers do to support each child in constructing thoughts, perceptions, beliefs, opinions, attitudes, and feelings? The simple yet multilayered answer is that teachers use their energy, intensity, and sensitivity to enrich, embolden, and enliven the learning environment for all students. They do so within the context of the following components:

1. Purposeful accessible learning
2. Confidence building
3. Spirit of collaboration/sense of pride
4. Creativity/imagination

While teachers have a great deal of control over affective variables that currently influence their students, they cannot alter a student's prior experiences nor build "new" prior knowledge. They *can*, however, create an environment so that each component is visible, viable, and intentionally palpable.

1. PURPOSEFUL ACCESSIBLE LEARNING

Think of a classroom and determine whether you can see, hear, and *feel* the energy as students either buzz around or settle in, ask questions, use models, become immersed in thought and engaged in conversation as they form new perceptions, ideas, and beliefs. Do you get the sense that there is a plan and a purpose for each student's actions? Has each one been set to a task that requires him to use what he already knows, to push himself and others a bit further as he makes new meaning and new learning? If so, then you know that this teacher has set purposeful learning into motion by presenting mathematical tasks that will bring about new learning, solidify prior learning, and do so with clarity and intentionality. As you move through this type of classroom, you can actually feel the classroom flashing the message that what all students are doing is important and that everyone has been invited to be a part of that vibrant community.

Students in such classrooms see and believe that mathematics serves a purpose that extends beyond just learning it for a test or grade. I love to use Margaret Wise Brown's *The Important Book* (1949) to set the stage for talking about general topics as well as specific topics such as math. After reading the book aloud, students complete several prompts based on the book. I find the results telling:

The important thing about math is . . .
. . . you learn all the time with it. (Naomi, Grade 2)
. . . it makes you think. (Corey, Grade 2)

. . . you need it to succeed in life. (Caleb, Grade 5)

. . . you can use it in any job, at any time, on any day. (Soshana, Grade 5)

It's like . . .

. . . a ride because sometimes it's bumpy and sometimes it's smooth. (Nuni, Grade 2)

. . . a slide because when you get on it, you can think and learn really fast. (Caroline, Grade 3)

. . . getting a gift because you can always use it. (Sari, Grade 4)

. . . a hole in the ground—it's endless and you will need it everywhere you go. (Matt, Grade 5)

These students clearly know the purpose of their mathematics learning, and they know that mathematics is important. Their beliefs and understandings are visible in their writing, but even more important, you can feel their acknowledgment that math has a purpose in their classrooms: "It's the best because it takes us past the test!" (Javier, Grade 4).

2. CONFIDENCE BUILDING

You know it when you see it—a risk-free environment that leads to greater learning, which then leads to greater confidence in students. Can you feel that this is a place where the teacher actively sets the stage for students to take risks so that their confidence continues to grow? Or is the teacher working from a deficit model of student learning, finding out what students don't know without using that information to foster their learning? On the other hand, do you get the impression that the teacher is more interested in providing multiple opportunities for students to show and tell what they know and can do without fear of being wrong? Further, can students discern this feeling? Do they believe and feel that their teacher views them with respect, assumes that all of them are capable learners, and wants to know what and how they think? It is easy to identify a classroom where students know that taking risks in their learning is not only accepted but also celebrated.

Recently, I was in a fourth-grade classroom observing an algebraic reasoning lesson. I watched with delight as this somewhat shy student came out with: "I understand how Nitzan figured out that one sphere equals two prisms, but I don't get how he solved the rest of the problem." Other students nodded their heads as she spoke. You could almost see her being lifted by support, knowing that it was acceptable for her to express her confusion. The classroom teacher had obviously done her job in establishing a trust between her and her students as well as among her students. These students felt safe putting themselves out there. As a result, they were more likely to push out a bit in their zones of proximal development (Vygotsky), to be knocked into a sense of disequilibrium (Piaget) so that new learning took place while wrapped in the knowledge that it was safe for them to do so.

As I entered a different fourth-grade classroom, I saw another wonderful example of how a student's confidence can grow when supported in the right way. Bethany was explaining to her teacher, Jaime Miller, how she could multiply 24 by 36 by thinking about it in terms of combinations (Figure 6.1). It was fabulous to watch Bethany move through the steps of her thinking with a newfound assurance. (See Figure 6.2 to follow her thought process.)

Figure 6.1: Fourth-grader Bethany exudes confidence as she explains her work to her teacher.

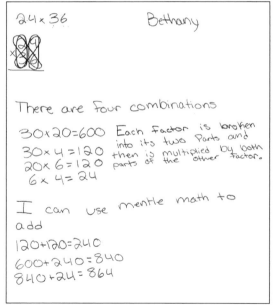

Figure 6.2: Bethany's explanation of how to multiply with two-digit numbers

Figure 6.3 shows a student's assessment of her performance in a fraction unit the class had just completed. She is able to explain some of the content she learned and how her knowledge level moved from a 5 to a 10 and conveys her feelings as a mathematical learner.

Students in these kinds of classrooms proceed with confidence and grow as a result.

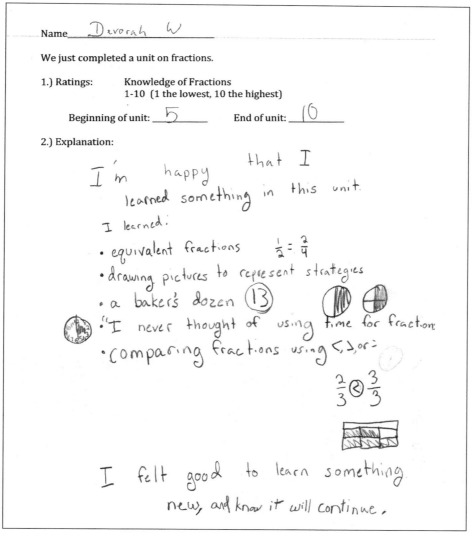

Name __Devorah W__

We just completed a unit on fractions.

1.) Ratings: Knowledge of Fractions
                1-10 (1 the lowest, 10 the highest)

    Beginning of unit: ___5___   End of unit: ___10___

2.) Explanation:

I'm happy that I learned something in this unit.

I learned:

• equivalent fractions $\frac{1}{2} = \frac{2}{4}$

• drawing pictures to represent strategies

• a baker's dozen ⑬

• "I never thought of using time for fraction"

• comparing fractions using <, >, or =

$\frac{2}{3} < \frac{3}{3}$

I felt good to learn something new, and know it will continue.

Figure 6.3: A student's self-assessment

3. SPIRIT OF COLLABORATION/SENSE OF PRIDE

Think of a classroom, and determine whether it is a place where students collaborate with one another. Do you sense that students support one another in their learning? Are they listening to what other students have to say and then offering positive feedback, building on ideas to move forward together? If you see this, it has not come about by accident. It is the result of the calculated and consistent work of the teacher, who has convinced her students that collaborating only makes them stronger and better learners.

Continuing to move through this classroom, can you perceive that the students have both a collective and an individual sense of accomplishment? Can you discern that they care about their work, whether it is done individually or with a partner (Figure 6.4) and that they attend to it with precision and accuracy? Can you observe them as they sigh or smile with satisfaction when they complete a task? Is their feeling of accomplishment detectable when they finish an explanation or model their thinking? If you are aware of these elements, then the teacher is responsible for setting expectations in such a way that, when the students work collaboratively to attain a goal, their sense of accomplishment is conspicuous.

Figure 6.5 shows the work of four fifth-grade students. They had been assigned the task of looking for the relationship between square numbers and the product of their neighbors (for example, $8^2 = 64$, $9 \times 7 = 63$, $10 \times 6 = 60$, etc.). The task was challenging, and yet they were able to solve it by working together and collaborating throughout the process. At the end of the task, the students had to record not only what they learned mathemati-

Figure 6.4: In true collaborative fashion, these second graders work together to solve the problem.

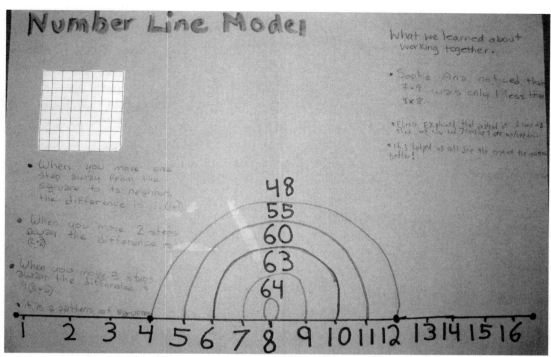

Figure 6.5: Learning through collaboration

cally but also what they learned about working together. It is evident that they were supremely proud of the results of their collaboration and had a clear sense of accomplishment. This is indeed a classroom in which every student is supported enough to accomplish meaningful tasks, thus setting a cyclical process into effect. Greater pride and accomplishment build self-esteem, allowing students to take more risks that bring about greater learning—a win-win for all!

4. CREATIVITY/IMAGINATION

Creativity and imagination send my heart soaring when I see them, hear them, and *feel* them in a classroom. I am aware of them when I see a student come up with a strategy that no one else has thought of and shares it with the class. I recognize them when I watch two students go off on a tangent because one of them asked, "What would happen if we did this?" I identify it when a reluctant participant asks, "Does this always work?" and then accepts the challenge of finding out whether it does.

Creativity in mathematics can hold different meanings. Some people have an aesthetic connection and think of creativity as reflected in tessellations and other artistic renderings of mathematical ideas and principles. I take a broader view of it and am more aligned with Derek Haylock who defines creativity in mathematics as "identified by overcoming fixations and rigidity in thinking; by divergent thinking, fluency, flexibility and originality in the generation of responses to mathematical situations" (2010, 50). This is the essence of powerful mathematical thinking—when students move beyond a fixed set of rules and procedures and diverge from a "safe" route to an answer on an often rocky road of discovery.

Roger Penrose, the renowned mathematical physicist who has worked with Stephen Hawking, speaks often about the importance of imagination in mathematics. He sees imagination as integral to mathematics and connects it to ancient Greeks who practiced that to prove something true is to imagine it as false and then look for a counterexample of sorts—a contradiction—that points to the truth. This represents divergent thinking as well as flexibility and originality. To see evidence of Penrose's imagination in mathematics, take a look at his "staircases" in some of M. C. Escher's work!

Let's look at fourth-grader Jonah's work here on fractions (Figure 6.6) and examine how he puzzled out a relationship between numerators and denominators. The class had been working on comparing and ordering fractions. Jonah approached his teacher with a unique strategy for comparing fractions that looked at the difference between the numerator and denominator in each fraction. He conjectured that the fraction with the smaller difference is the larger of the two fractions.

The teacher was not sure whether Jonah's thinking was correct and allowed him to see her uncertainty. She had sent him to the school's math specialist with whom I was working that day so that Ms. Munro could see his work because, in Jonah's words, "My teacher called this great! She said it is out-of-the-box thinking but she wants to see if you think it makes sense." Jonah was clearly proud that his work had sparked this kind of response—that he had "stumped" his teacher, that he had thought of something no one else in his class had thought of, and that he had discovered something unique. Even though Ms. Munro worked with Jonah and eventually together they found counterexamples that disproved his conjecture, the evidence of his creative and original thinking was celebrated by all.

This component—creativity/imagination must be watered daily by the teacher if it is to take root and grow. While most of us see that part of mathematics is logical thinking and careful reasoning, mathematics is also linked

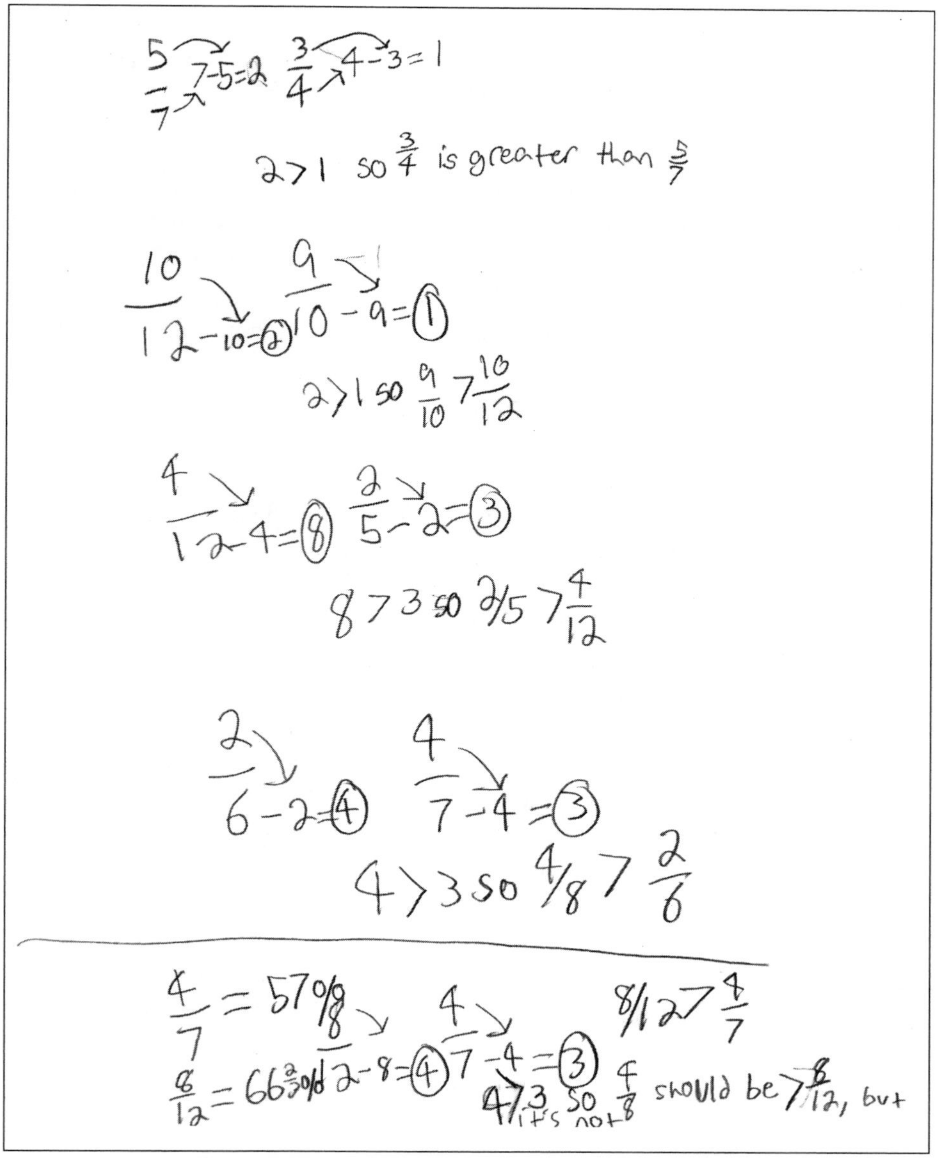

$$\frac{5}{7} \quad 7-5=2 \qquad \frac{3}{4} \quad 4-3=1$$

$2 > 1$ so $\frac{3}{4}$ is greater than $\frac{5}{7}$

$$\frac{10}{12} \quad 12-10=2 \qquad \frac{9}{10} \quad 10-9=1$$

$2 > 1$ so $\frac{9}{10} > \frac{10}{12}$

$$\frac{4}{12} \quad 12-4=8 \qquad \frac{2}{5} \quad 5-2=3$$

$8 > 3$ so $\frac{2}{5} > \frac{4}{12}$

$$\frac{2}{6} \quad 6-2=4 \qquad \frac{4}{7} \quad 7-4=3$$

$4 > 3$ so $\frac{4}{8} > \frac{2}{6}$

$$\frac{4}{7} = 57\% \quad \frac{4}{8} \qquad \frac{8}{12} > \frac{4}{7}$$

$$\frac{8}{12} = 66\frac{2}{3}\% \quad 12-8=4 \qquad \frac{4}{7} \quad 7-4=3$$

$4 > 3$ so $\frac{4}{8}$ should be $> \frac{8}{12}$, but it's not

Figure 6.6: Jonah's creative thinking about the relationship between numerators and denominators

to the creative parts of our minds. This is where our imaginations take us, pushing us in various directions, allowing us to test our thoughts, envisioning new and original ways. Albert Einstein said it beautifully: "Logic will get you from A to B. Imagination will take you everywhere."

INTENSIFICATION: A TALE OF TWO CLASSROOMS

For the past few months, I have been doing professional development work with a group of prekindergarten through eighth-grade teachers. Over time, I have come to know them within the confines of our shared work, but recently I was able to get into some of their classrooms. As a result, I got to peel away at the pomegranate and found lots of "delightful tidbits"!

The fourth-grade classroom I visited gave off an undeniable sense of energy immediately. The teacher, Mrs. Nicholson, had just called the students to the meeting area for a group lesson. The announcement was met with scattered positive responses ("Yay!" "Oh, good. Time for math!"). It was great to hear excitement about an impending math lesson rather than the negative responses sometimes heard. Mrs. Nicholson began by having one of the students read the lesson goals: (1) to analyze bar graphs and circle graphs and (2) to draw conclusions and answer questions from the data. She asked for definitions, examples, and opinions. Every student spoke during this time, either to a partner or to the class. Mrs. Nicholson's low-key, matter-of-fact manner may have conveyed her expectation that the lesson was for everyone and that all would be held accountable. Every student knew the purpose of the lesson and what to do. As the students moved to complete the task in partner groups, I listened in:

Felipe: I think I have an idea about how to solve the first one.
Malea: I think I do, too. What's yours?
Felipe: If we put all the information in a table first, we can see what we have.
Malea: Yeah, and then we can decide which way to show it is best.
Mrs. Nicholson (who had just come over to the pair): I like the way you both had a similar idea about how and where to start. Great idea. Now tell me why this is a good thing to do.

It was clear from these students' reactions that they felt comfortable answering Mrs. Nicholson. She had already buoyed their confidence by acknowledging that their idea was good and then followed up with the message that she knew they could justify their decision making. Further, by making the result of the students' task the creation of one "best" representation of their combined thinking, Mrs. Nicholson was increasing the likelihood that partners would have to collaborate with one another—a win-win situation.

As I walked around the classroom, I saw similar scenes everywhere. Each student was working on the task. Yes, it was easier for some than for others, but all kept working, seeking help from one another as well as from Mrs. Nicholson. Everyone worked purposefully, exhibiting confidence in his ability as well as in the ability of his partner. Satisfaction and pride emerged as each partner group completed the task and brought their results to the lesson summation meeting, ready, willing, and able to share with the class.

Soon after this, I went into Mrs. Adamson's kindergarten classroom. As I walked in, I was struck by how different it was from the fourth-grade class-room and not in the way you might expect. It was quieter, darker, more sub-dued, but it took about a minute, however, to realize that this class was humming along in much the same way as the fourth-grade class. Students were spread out in six different areas working on different tasks. A group in the math center was replicating shapes with pattern blocks, with varying degrees of difficulty. Two sets of partner groups were playing an addition card game and recording their work. Three students were in the reading cen-ter, reading math books, and each student shared her book with others. Three other students worked on a number-squeeze activity (one of them act-ing as the teacher) in the general meeting area. Four students sat with the teacher at a kidney-shaped table playing a subtraction game using dice. Another partner group reviewed the class math question of the day and worked on coming up with different ways to solve the problem.

I was pulled into this room and instantly "felt" all of the components that made this a place where rich mathematics happens for each student. Talk about purposeful and accessible. Every student was actively engaged in an activity that was either establishing, reinforcing, or extending his learn-ing. The air crackled with confidence. I saw students approach a task in more than one way, taking risks, and feeling as though this was within reach. If they did not solve a problem the first time, they tried it again. Watching them help one another and work together to complete the pattern block puzzles, to play the addition game, to give "hints" to help with number squeeze, I witnessed the spirit of collaboration that permeated the room and the sense of pride in jobs well done. Add to that the joy that was felt when Mariana and Gabriella, who were working on a different way to solve the math question of the day, came up with a completely different solution path. Top this off with Ahmed's announcement that "I used my imagination to see what this shape looked like doubled up and then I made it!" His five-sided star made from hexagons, rhombi, and triangle pattern blocks was a perfect doubled expansion of the one on the task card. Ahmed was beaming as his group responded with oohs, ahs, and wows!

Although identifying components that describe how a thriving mathematics classroom should *feel* might offer a challenge, it is well worth the time. When you walk through your or someone else's classroom, you can tell whether you are in an environment where students and teachers love to learn mathematics, because these components are tangible and palpable. This love of learning math is evident in the purposeful learning that sets the classroom humming as students and teachers perform meaningful tasks. It is there when you can feel that all students believe that this is *their* classroom and that they are a vital part of this community. It is there when you can sense that students, who might otherwise be reluctant to take a chance and risk being wrong, feel secure to take risks that are celebrated. As a result, their confidence swells. The love is boosted even more when students pulsate with collective and individual pride in their accomplishments, fueled by the spirit of collaboration and cooperation. The icing on the cake is when you can feel the sparks that come from creativity and wonderment, imagination and awe. You know you are in a classroom where students believe that they and their ideas are important.

Some components of math "sense"—what should be seen, heard, and felt in mathematics classrooms—have been discussed throughout this book. But where does one start? Let's move to Chapter 7 for more suggestions.

CHAPTER

7

PUTTING IT TOGETHER

To get through the hardest journey we need take only one step at a time,
but we must keep on stepping.

—Chinese Proverb

I have spoken a great deal about how we as educators are on a journey, constantly taking steps to improve, refine, and extend our teaching so that we can improve, refine, and extend the learning of our students. Educators are charged with an awesome responsibility; one most of us accept. Even though the journey can be hard at times, it is packed enough with joy to empower us to "keep on stepping."

In thinking about how to use this book, a good place to begin is to take stock of where you are now on your journey so that you can chart the next steps. Knowing where you want to go and finding your "You Are Here" location on a map are usually the first steps of any trip. Once you are clear about the beginning and the ending places, then you can plan how to get there and which routes to take.

I've said that good mathematics teaching and learning cannot be reduced to a checklist. I stand by that. There is, however, an advantage to standing still, taking stock, and finding where you are before you make the next move. The self-assessments that follow present components of this book to help you pinpoint your individualized You Are Here location so that you can plan your personal itinerary. (You will find reproducibles in the Appendix.) Included are some thoughts and suggestions for completion and use.

These checklists should be used to catalyze thinking about the elements of effective instruction. The caveat from previous chapters must also be repeated here—the mere presence of these components, especially the physical ones, does not necessarily equate with appropriate and effective use. Checklists are intended for teacher reflection and collaboration among colleagues, rather than for evaluation.

THE LOOK OF THE LANDSCAPE

- This is a good place to start, as it is relatively easy to complete.
- Look around your room specifically for the ten components listed. If the item is present, place a check in the column.
- If it is present, think about how often you use it and place a number in the Frequency of Use column according to the given scale.
- If it is present and you use it, determine how well you use it and place a number in the Quality of Use column in accordance with the given scale.
- Add to the Comments column any information that may be useful as you devise an action plan (e.g., used to use it but got out of the habit; is on order already; need to access resource to learn how to use it).

THE LOOK OF THE LANDSCAPE SELF-ASSESSMENT

Date: _____

Component	Present	Frequency of Use	Quality of Use	Comments
	(if present, complete next two columns)	1. Rarely 2. Sometimes 3. Often 4. Consistently	1. Beginning 2. Adequate 3. Strong 4. Optimal	
number line				
100 chart/ number grid				
manipulatives				
student work samples				
daily schedule				
designated math center				
math word wall				
math literature collection				
technology				
multiple instructional settings				

THE LOOK OF THE LESSON: TEACHERS

- Look at the components of this assessment in advance of completing it and allow time to reflect on what each means to you.
- Think about how often you can see yourself doing these actions or moves. Place a number in the Frequency of Use column according to the given scale.
- Determine where you see yourself, what stage you are in on the continuum in terms of how well you execute/perform these components. Place a number in the Quality of Use column in accordance with the given scale.
- Add to the Comments column any information that may be useful as you devise an action plan (e.g., have some good resources but need to review them; don't know enough about how to do this; should think about asking [trusted colleague] to observe me).

THE LOOK OF THE LESSON: STUDENTS

- Look at the components of this assessment in advance of completing it and allow time to reflect on what each means to you.
- Think about how often you can see students in your classroom engaged in these components. Place a number in the Frequency of Use column according to the given scale.
- Determine where you see yourself on the continuum in your stage of understanding as well as your ability to support students so that they can execute/perform these components. Place a number in the Quality of Use column in accordance with the given scale.
- Add to the Comments column any information that may be useful as you devise an action plan (e.g., no resources/need to get some; they did this earlier in the year but are no longer doing so; should think about asking [trusted colleague] if I can observe him).

THE LOOK OF THE LESSON SELF-ASSESSMENT: TEACHERS

Date:

Component	Present (if present, complete next two columns)	Frequency of Use 1. Rarely 2. Sometimes 3. Often 4. Consistently	Quality of Use 1. Beginning 2. Adequate 3. Strong 4. Optimal	Comments
differentiating instruction				
checking for understanding				
facilitating mathematical thinking				
identifying student misconceptions				
providing written feedback				
using wait time				
setting & sharing lesson goals/ objectives				

THE LOOK OF THE LESSON SELF-ASSESSMENT: STUDENTS

Date: _____

Component	Present	Frequency of Use	Quality of Use	Comments
	(if present, complete next two columns)	1. Rarely 2. Sometimes 3. Often 4. Consistently	1. Beginning 2. Adequate 3. Strong 4. Optimal	
actively engaging				
actively listening				
collaborating				
making connections				
persevering				
using what they know to find what they don't know				
taking risks				

THE SOUND OF THE LESSON: TEACHERS/STUDENTS/BOTH

- The components for "The Sound of the Lesson" have been placed in one self-assessment chart. Look at the components of this assessment in advance and allow yourself time to reflect on what each means to you.
- For the teacher components, think about how often you can hear yourself engaged in these actions or moves. Place a number in the Frequency of Use column according to the given scale.
- Determine where you see yourself, what stage you are in on the continuum in terms of how well you execute/perform these components. Place a number in the Quality of Use column in accordance with the given scale.
- For the student components, think about how often you hear students in your classroom engaged in these components. Place a number in the Frequency of Use column according to the given scale.
- Determine where you see yourself on the continuum in your stage of understanding as well as your ability to support students so that they can execute/perform these components. Place a number in the Quality of Use column in accordance with the given scale.
- Follow the same procedure for the components ascribed to both teachers and students.
- Add to the Comments column any information that may be useful as you devise an action plan (e.g., have some good resources but need to review them; don't know enough about how to do this; should think about asking [trusted colleague] to observe me).

THE SOUND OF THE LESSON SELF-ASSESSMENT: TEACHERS/STUDENTS/BOTH

Date:_____

Component	Present (if present, complete next two columns)	Frequency of Use 1. Rarely 2. Sometimes 3. Often 4. Consistently	Quality of Use 1. Beginning 2. Adequate 3. Strong 4. Optimal	Comments
T: supporting discourse				
T: providing lesson summary/reflection				
T: engaging all students				
S: justifying & clarifying their thinking				
S: analyzing the thinking of others				
Both: actively listening				
Both: encouraging & modeling risk taking				
Both: using mathematical vocabulary				

THE FEEL OF IT ALL

- Look at the components of this assessment in advance and allow yourself time to reflect on what each means to you.
- Think about how often you can "feel" these components in your classroom. Place a number in the Frequency of Use column according to the given scale.
- Determine where you see yourself, what stage you are in on the continuum in how well you foster, nurture, and support these components. Place a number in the Quality of Use column in accordance with the given scale.
- Add to the Comments column useful information to help you devise an action plan.

THE FEEL OF IT ALL SELF-ASSESSMENT

Date:

Component	Present (if present, complete next two columns)	Frequency of Use 1. Rarely 2. Sometimes 3. Often 4. Consistently	Quality of Use 1. Beginning 2. Adequate 3. Strong 4. Optimal	Comments
purposeful accessible learning				
confidence building				
spirit of collaboration/ sense of pride				
creativity/ imagination				

NEXT STEPS

1. Self-Assessments:
   - Find a chunk of time and complete the self-assessments for Chapters 2, 3, 4, and 5.
   - Choose one (or two) components from each chapter that you would like to focus on first. Alternatively, you may decide that you would like to concentrate on the chapters one at a time and work on related components.
   - Knowing where you are and where you want to get to, choose a route to get there. A few suggestions follow.

2. Support from Colleagues:
   - Peer coaching is a great way to move along in this work. Partner with a trusted colleague and help each other by meeting with and observing each other with specific targets in mind. In follow-up meetings, discuss where to go from there.
   - Professional learning communities (PLCs) are a more formal way for teachers to come together to improve student learning. Elements from this book can be used as the basis for some PLC work.
   - Book groups offer another way to share thinking and learning. This book can be used as an anchor for a grade-level team, a cross-level group, or an entire school.

3. Support from Administrators:
   - Building or district mathematics specialists/coaches/supervisors can be sources of support in a variety of ways. They can provide materials or the resources to purchase materials. They can facilitate your use of materials by grounding them in mathematical purpose. Further, these specialists can observe and coach you (not evaluate) and then can help you sharpen your focus and goals with constructive feedback.
   - Building principals are another potential source of support. You may decide to share your goals with your principal and enlist him or her as a companion on your journey.

However you decide to use this book, I hope your math sense is heightened and that you are more aware of the look, the sound, and the feel of a mathematics classroom that supports each student. Teaching is hard work. As Abigail Adams once said, "Learning is not attained by chance. It must be sought for with ardor and attended to with diligence."

Teachers know that learning does not just happen. No magic fairies come to sprinkle learning dust on our students. Teachers are filled with passion and ardor, sustained by a seemingly unending well of conscientiousness and diligence. Teaching is about taking steps toward the goal of igniting a love for learning—in this case mathematics—that will serve students well and allow them to think of themselves as capable mathematical thinkers, open to the endless possibilities before them.

APPENDIX

SELF-ASSESSMENTS

THE LOOK OF THE LANDSCAPE SELF-ASSESSMENT

Date: _____

Component	Present	Frequency of Use	Quality of Use	Comments
	(if present, complete next two columns)	1. Rarely 2. Sometimes 3. Often 4. Consistently	1. Beginning 2. Adequate 3. Strong 4. Optimal	
number line				
100 chart/ number grid				
manipulatives				
student work samples				
daily schedule				
designated math center				
math word wall				
math literature collection				
technology				
multiple instructional settings				

THE LOOK OF THE LESSON SELF-ASSESSMENT: TEACHERS

Date:_____

Component	Present (if present, complete next two columns)	Frequency of Use 1. Rarely 2. Sometimes 3. Often 4. Consistently	Quality of Use 1. Beginning 2. Adequate 3. Strong 4. Optimal	Comments
differentiating instruction				
checking for understanding				
facilitating mathematical thinking				
identifying student misconceptions				
providing written feedback				
using wait time				
setting & sharing lesson goals/ objectives				

THE LOOK OF THE LESSON SELF-ASSESSMENT: STUDENTS

Date:_____

Component	Present	Frequency of Use	Quality of Use	Comments
	(if present, complete next two columns)	1. Rarely 2. Sometimes 3. Often 4. Consistently	1. Beginning 2. Adequate 3. Strong 4. Optimal	
actively engaging				
actively listening				
collaborating				
making connections				
persevering				
using what they know to find what they don't know				
taking risks				

THE SOUND OF THE LESSON SELF-ASSESSMENT: TEACHERS/STUDENTS/BOTH

Date:_____

Component	Present (if present, complete next two columns)	Frequency of Use 1. Rarely 2. Sometimes 3. Often 4. Consistently	Quality of Use 1. Beginning 2. Adequate 3. Strong 4. Optimal	Comments
T: supporting discourse				
T: providing lesson summary/ reflection				
T: engaging all students				
S: justifying & clarifying their thinking				
S: analyzing the thinking of others				
Both: actively listening				
Both: encourag- ing & modeling risk taking				
Both: using mathematical vocabulary				

THE FEEL OF IT ALL SELF-ASSESSMENT

Date: _____

Component	Present	Frequency of Use	Quality of Use	Comments
	(if present, complete next two columns)	1. Rarely 2. Sometimes 3. Often 4. Consistently	1. Beginning 2. Adequate 3. Strong 4. Optimal	
purposeful accessible learning				
confidence building				
spirit of collaboration/ sense of pride				
creativity/ imagination				

REFERENCES

Bamberger, Honi, Christine Oberdorf, and Karren Schultz-Ferrell. 2010. *Math Misconceptions, Pre-K–Grade 5: From Misunderstanding to Deep Understanding.* Portsmouth, NH: Heinemann.

Barnett-Clarke, Carne, and Alma Ramirez. 2004. "Language Pitfalls and Pathways to Mathematics." In *Perspectives on the Teaching of Mathematics,* ed. Rheta N. Rubenstein, 56–66. Reston, VA: National Council of Teachers of Mathematics.

Bezuszka, Stanley. 1993. *From Heart and Mind: A Classroom Odyssey.* Palo Alto, CA: Dale Seymour.

Boykin, A. Wade, and Boyd Noguera. 2011. *Creating the Opportunity to Learn.* Alexandria, VA: ASCD.

Brookhart, Susan. 2008. *How to Give Effective Feedback to Your Students.* Alexandria, VA: ASCD.

Brown, Margaret Wise. 1949. *The Important Book.* New York: HarperCollins.

Bunting, Eve. 1996. *Market Day.* New York: HarperCollins.

California Department of Education. 2012. *Recommended Literature for Science & Mathematics.* Sacramento, CA: California Department of Education. Available online at http://www.cde.ca.gov/ci/sc/ll/.

Chapin, Suzanne H., Catherine O'Connor, and Nancy Canavan Anderson. 2009. *Classroom Discussions: Using Math Talk to Help Students Learn.* Sausalito, CA: Math Solutions.

Common Core State Standards Initiative. 2010. *Common Core State Standards for Mathematics.* Washington, DC: National Governors Association Center for Best Practices and the Council of Chief State School Officers. http://www .corestandards.org/the-standards.

Dacey, Linda, and Anne Collins. 2010/2011. Zeroing in on Number and Operations: Key Ideas and Common Misconceptions, Grades Pre-K–8. Portland, ME: Stenhouse.

Dacey, Linda, and Karen Gartland. 2009. *Math for All: Differentiating Instruction, Grades 6–8*. Sausalito, CA: Math Solutions.

Dacey, Linda, and Jayne Lynch. 2007. *Math for All: Differentiating Instruction, Grades 3–5*. Sausalito, CA: Math Solutions.

Dacey, Linda, and Rebeka Eston Salemi. 2007. *Math for All: Differentiating Instruction, Grades K–2*. Sausalito, CA: Math Solutions.

Duckworth, Eleanor. 1996. *"The Having of Wonderful Ideas" and Other Essays on Teaching and Learning*. 2nd ed. New York: Teachers College Press.

Freire, Paolo. 2000. *Pedagogy of the Oppressed*. 30th anniversary ed. New York: Continuum International Publishing Group.

Haylock, Derek. 2010. *Mathematics Explained for Primary Teachers*. 4th ed. Thousand Oaks, CA: Sage.

Himmele, Persida, and William Himmele. 2011. *Total Participation Techniques: Making Every Student an Active Learner*. Alexandria, VA: ASCD.

Hunter, Madeline. 1982. *Master Teaching*. El Segundo, CA: TIP.

Marzano, Robert, and Debra J. Pickering. 2005. *Building Academic Vocabulary*. Alexandria, VA: ASCD.

National Council of Teachers of Mathematics. 2000. *Principles and Standards for School Mathematics*. Reston, VA: National Council of Teachers of Mathematics.

————.2006. *Curriculum Focal Points for Prekindergarten Through Grade 8 Mathematics: A Quest for Coherence*. Reston, VA: National Council of Teachers of Mathematics.

Omohundro Wedekind, Kassia. 2011. *Math Exchanges: Guiding Young Mathematicians in Small-Group Meetings*. Portland, ME: Stenhouse.

Piaget, Jean. 1959. *The Language and Thought of the Child*. 3rd ed. London: Routledge and Kegan Paul.

Polya, George. 1945. *How to Solve It*. Princeton, NJ: Princeton University.

Rathouz, Margaret. 2011. "3 Ways That Promote Student Reasoning." *Teaching Children Mathematics* 18 (3): 182–189.

Rowe, Mary Budd. 1986. "Wait Time: Slowing Down May Be a Way of Speeding Up!" *Journal of Teacher Education* 37 (1): 43–50.

Saphier, Jon, Mary Ann Haley-Speca, and Robert Gower. 2008. *The Skillful Teacher: Building Your Teaching Skills*. 6th ed. Acton, MA: Research for Better Teaching.

Tang, Greg. 2001. *The Grapes of Math*. New York: Scholastic.

Tobin, Kenneth. 1987. "The Role of Wait Time in Higher Cognitive Level Learning." *Review of Educational Research* 57 (1): 69–95.

Tomlinson, Carol Ann, and Marcia B. Imbeau. 2010. *Leading and Managing a Differentiated Classroom*. Alexandria, VA: ASCD.

Vygotsky, Lev S. 1978. *Mind in Society*. Cambridge, MA: Harvard University Press.

Wiggins, Grant, and Jay McTighe. 1998. *Understanding by Design*. Alexandria, VA: ASCD.

INDEX

Page numbers followed by an *f* indicate figures.